"Analytically brilliant; crystal clear w
its investigation; entertaining and eru
to know what the alternative to auste.
better guide."

Danny Dorling, University of Oxford

"John Weeks is one of the most incisive critics of austerity policy. In this book he shows, in clear, non-technical
language, how the mythology of 'balancing the books'
has subverted public understanding of the social and
economic purpose of state budgets, allowing governments to inflict serious, unnecessary and possibly lasting
damage on ordinary citizens."

Lord Robert Skidelsky, Warwick University and the
British Academy

"John Weeks is a distinguished and worldly economist
who, long before it became fashionable, rigorously, and
to devastating effect, contested the intellectual foundations of neoliberal economics. His generosity in sharing
his deep knowledge of economic theory, policies and
systems has inspired and motivated many thousands of
students, policy makers and activists. His work in discrediting the policies of austerity laid the foundations
on which Labour's Corbyn movement was built and
popularized."

Ann Pettifor, Director, Prime Economics

"Austerity is one of the greatest deceptions foisted on
the British public in modern history. It was based on

ideological economics designed to accelerate the dismantling of the social state and the privatization of the commons. John Weeks has been a consistent principled critic since the austerity era was launched. His scorn should be welcomed."

Guy Standing, SOAS, University of London

"John Weeks has been one of the most powerful critics of mainstream neoclassical economics and of neoliberal economic policies in the last few decades. His analyses are razor-sharp and his criticisms unsparing, but he uses them to propose ways to build a solidaristic economy and a compassionate society."

Ha-Joon Chang, University of Cambridge

"John Weeks has been a vigorous campaigner against the fallacies of neoliberal economics. He is a model to us all in his energy and resilience in making the case for a more progressive economics and promoting an alternative approach to economic policy making that is sorely needed. He draws on his long and valuable experience in teaching, research and advising governments around the world. It is a tribute to his influence and his clarity of exposition that his students are now taking his ideas forward both at home and abroad."

Susan Himmelweit, Open University

# The Debt Delusion

For my son Matthew Dore-Weeks

# The Debt Delusion

## Living Within Our Means and Other Fallacies

John F. Weeks

polity

First published in 2020 by Polity Press

Reprinted 2020

Polity Press
65 Bridge Street
Cambridge CB2 1UR, UK

Polity Press
101 Station Landing
Suite 300
Medford, MA 02155, USA

ISBN-13: 978-1-5095-3293-3
ISBN-13: 978-1-5095-3294-0 (pb)

A catalogue record for this book is available from the British Library.

Library of Congress Cataloging-in-Publication Data

Names: Weeks, John, 1941- author.
Title: The debt delusion : living within our means and other fallacies / John Weeks.
Description: Cambridge, UK ; Medford, MA : Polity Press, 2019. | Includes bibliographical references and index.
Identifiers: LCCN 2019016223 (print) | LCCN 2019018253 (ebook) | ISBN 9781509532964 (Epub) | ISBN 9781509532933 (hardback) | ISBN 9781509532940 (pbk.)
Subjects: LCSH: Debts, Public. | Finance, Public. | Government spending policy. | Fiscal policy.
Classification: LCC HJ8015 (ebook) | LCC HJ8015 .W44 2019 (print) | DDC 336.3/4--dc23
LC record available at https://lccn.loc.gov/2019016223

Typeset in 11 on 14 pt Sabon by
Servis Filmsetting Ltd, Stockport, Cheshire
Printed and bound in Great Britain by TJ Books Limited

For further information on Polity, visit our website: politybooks.com

# Contents

# Table and Figures

# Table and Figures

# Table and Figures

# Introduction: Debt, Deficits and Austerity

## A Citizen's Guide

In the second stanza of Lewis Carroll's *The Hunting of the Snark*, the Bellman tells the rest of the ship's crew, "I have said it thrice: What I tell you three times is true." This propaganda technique of repetition establishes familiarity then credibility even to obvious contractions of reality. The austerity narrative – governments should spend no more than their tax incomes – provides powerful proof of the effectiveness of repletion to give myth credibility.

Central to the general acceptance of myths about government budgets is lack of basic understanding by citizens of public spending and taxation. Lack of understanding becomes misunderstanding under the assault of propaganda and provides fertile soil for converting myth into conventional wisdom (a term coined with analytical insight by the US economist and diplomat John Kenneth Galbraith). Knowledge provides the tool to expose myths as the non-credible parables they are, to reveal conventional wisdom as myth no matter how frequent the repetition.

Informed citizens provide the foundation of democratic society. Participating through democratic institutions, we the citizens facilitate effective government. Understanding government finances is central to that participation. Participation creates engagement, so that the citizen becomes the active subject of policy discussion rather than the passive object.

Ill-informed citizens fall prey to cynicism that undermines democratic participation by inducing alienated passivity. Through fostering the ignorance that generates cynicism, governments can rule on behalf of the special interests rather than for the general welfare. Governments serving the few neutralize and undermine democracy, claiming to bring order and stability to replace disorder and disarray – disorder and disarray typically generated by their special interest policies.

In both Europe and the United States, few public issues are as consistently misrepresented as government budgets. The misrepresentation facilitates policies that undermine rather than enhance the public welfare. To defend special interests, governments use these misrepresentations to justify policies that weaken the ability of the public to participate as citizens. Central to that weakening is the superficially reasonable proposition that, complex as it is, public finance should be left to experts. The final chapter of this book inspects this proposition and rejects it.

Misrepresentation and bogus appeal to experts distort public debate on how much governments should spend, how that spending should be funded, and who should benefit. As a result, a very large part of public discussion over government spending and tax does not inform. It misinforms and leaves citizens knowing less, not more, accepting myths as if they were common sense. Polemics marshal the language of myth to combat the wisdom and insight that facilitate democratic decision making.

A substantial part of the public hesitates from engaging in discussion of government budgets because of an imagined lack of expertise. Citizens retreat from what they believe is a complex subject, offering the plea "I am not an economist," and "Economics is too dull and difficult to try to understand." These laments result from the inculcation of misinformation through extensive and pervasive propaganda. Public-sector spending and taxation are overwhelmingly about politics and only secondarily about economics. Yet many politicians and much of the media discuss public finances as if the reverse were the case. Debates over political priorities are too frequently treated as if they were a technical matter for experts. The need for expertise in a democratic society is important and its role is clear – experts advise, politicians decide, and citizens elect.

This book takes the reader past superficial rhetoric for a straightforward discussion of "fiscal policy" – public spending, taxation, the balance between the two ("surpluses" and "deficits"), and the concrete function of all three. Reading this book requires no economic knowledge. I taught economics for over forty years, spending as much time dispelling the misleading conventional wisdom of the profession as I did presenting how economies actually work.

My commitment to non-technical language might appropriately begin with a bit on "jargon-busting" on budget language. The word "fiscal" has its origin in the

Latin word *fiscus*, meaning a bag, basket or purse for holding money. The word came to mean the Roman state treasury. Thus, "fiscal policy" has a simple meaning: management of the public purse.

With jargon banished, readers following my explanations require only the commitment to think logically and to link logic to what we observe, attributes common to all citizens. There is no mathematics here, and the arithmetic hardly goes beyond adding and subtracting. A problem we repeatedly face is that the words used in debates over public spending and taxation take on so much ideological baggage that they represent barriers to understanding. Foremost among these are "deficit" and "debt," whose meanings, measurement and policy significance are distorted by mutually reinforcing misrepresentations.

In Dutch and German the word for "debt" also means "guilt," which provides insight into the decades-old austerity policies of the German Ministry of Finance, as well as the deficit and debt rules in the treaties of the European Union. In English, "debt" and "guilt" are different words. Nonetheless, many English-speaking politicians, not least the former UK Chancellor George Osborne and former Republican Congressman Paul Ryan, use the former to imply a heavy dose of the latter. In some cases the transubstantiation of meaning brings memories of "Newspeak" in George Orwell's *1984*. A clear example is the use of the benign "savings" for the malign "cuts in public services" and the pejorative "black hole" for the neutral "revenue shortfall."

This book uses Citizenspeak rather than neo-Orwellian Newspeak to dispel rhetorical fallacies and lay the basis for informed public debate among knowledgeable citizens. This is a book by a citizen for other citizens aimed at demystifying public spending and taxation. To achieve that demystification we directly confront the myths that obscure understanding of what our government does. Foremost among these is the "living within our means" cliché (Myth 1), whose vagueness is its strength, allowing it to serve as an all-purpose justification for many fallacious arguments about public policy.

One of the most important messages spun off from "living within our means" is that governments should "balance their books" (Myth 2). The balancing metaphor is powerful and easily captures the mind, contrasting balance, a good thing, with imbalance and skewedness, which in the mind's eye cry out for correction just as a picture hanging crookedly offends the eye and demands adjustment.

The conventional narrative applies this metaphor of balance to the public budget because of its alleged validity for households. What reasonable person would challenge that households should balance their accounts? If we do not, "we must tighten our belts" (Myth 3). It is a mystery how this parable, "households must balance their books, so government should also," ever left the starting blocks, much less gained general acceptance. A bit of reflection and a few statistics lead unambiguously to quite a different parable.

Households do not "balance their books" as general practice. And when households spend more than their incomes they do not "tighten their belts" except when their circumstances are very dire. The making-ends-meet, balance-the-books, tighten-belts metaphors draw their legitimacy from the myth that debt is always bad (Myth 4). In *Hamlet*, the tediously pompous and much ridiculed Polonius encapsulates the debt myth when he tells his son, "Neither a borrower nor a lender be" (Act 1, scene 3). We find the modern Polonius manifested on a website named appropriately enough "The Balance" (www.thebalance.com). There we read, "A little debt won't hurt, will it?," followed by the ominous warning "That's how it starts," leading to profligate degeneracy and the disintegration of families. That almost no households practice debt abhorrence should come as a surprise to few, yet the fear of debt persists as conventional wisdom.

Because we must live within our means (Myth 1) and our government must do the same (Myth 2), we and our government must tighten our belts (Myth 3) and stay out of debt (Myth 4) by reducing expenditure, not raising taxes (Myth 5). We string the five myths together and come to the super-conclusion: there is "no alternative to austerity" (Myth 6).

All five of the building blocks used to construct the necessity of fiscal austerity are false (each is a myth). When we replace the myths with logic and reality, we reach the opposite conclusion, that "there is always an alternative." The closing chapter presents an alternative approach based on previous myth-busting. Reversing the rhetoric of the first myth, in the conclusion I show that, when we abandon the myths of austerity, our government can indeed "live within its means" while funding a just society. We have the means to foster hope over despair, infuse optimism in place of pessimism, imagine a brighter future and achieve it.

## *Austerity Politics*

As noted, in almost every country economic policy is more about politics than economics, though policy makers frequently employ technical economic arguments when justifying their political predilections. The use of esoteric technical language to convey political messages is not confided to economics. We frequently find it in discussions of public transport, education and health services. Somewhat unique to the politics of economic policy is the use of "common-sense" parables to convey political messages as if they were self-evident. The necessity of national governments to cover expenditure with tax revenue frequently stars as the central message of these parables.

Parables and myths have a long and analytically undistinguished history. In developed countries their influence and frequency declined substantially in the first three decades after World War II. The Great Depression of the 1930s and the subsequent need for a major government role in war-time economies made the limitations of "budget-balancing" metaphors obvious. After the war, both in the United States and in Europe, progressive parties favored a larger role for government, including a substantial spending share, while conservative parties preferred a more restricted and smaller public sector. The political preference for a small public sector tended not to place primary justification in arguments based on the necessity to match public spending with public revenue.

When discussing austerity and public budgets in general, a look at concrete experiences proves helpful, including inspection of statistics. Because national statistical offices do not always collect the same information, or when they do they do not present it in the same manner, a pragmatic approach is required. Throughout this book the analysis seeks to make comparisons, marshalling statistics from various countries, chosen for relevance to the issue under inspection. Effort is made to compare like with like, and this frequently restricts which countries can be compared.

The practice of public budgeting, in contrast to the rhetoric, is shown in figures 0.1 and 0.2, first for the United States, followed by the United Kingdom. Over the seven decades 1950 to 2018, the US federal government accounts showed an overall deficit in sixty of the sixty-eight years. Consecutive years without deficits occurred only twice, in 1956–7, when Dwight Eisenhower served as president, and from 1998 to 2001, during the presidency of Bill Clinton. The average for the seven decades was minus 2.2 percent of national

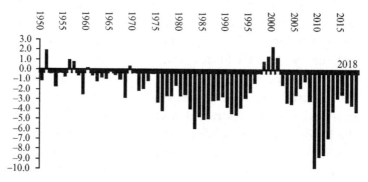

*Figure 0.1 Public revenue minus spending for the United States, 1950–2018, percentage of gross domestic product*

Source: Annual *Economic Report of the President*, historical tables.

8

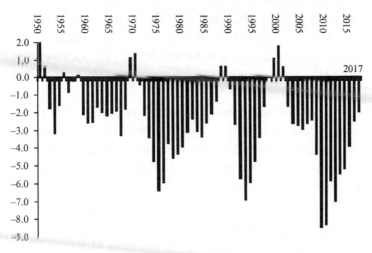

*Figure 0.2 Public revenue minus spending for the United Kingdom, 1950–2017, percentage of gross domestic product*

Source: UK Office for National Statistics.

income (gross national product). In practice, neither Democrat nor Republican presidential administrations considered it a problem requiring immediate correction when spending exceeded tax revenue, though rhetoric might have been otherwise. Governments of US neighbor Canada have shown a greater tendency to surpluses, though far from half the time, in eleven of the fifty-seven years between 1960 and 2017 (all consecutive, 1998–2008).

Over the same seven decades as in figure 0.1, the government of the United Kingdom consistently oversaw negative outcomes in the balance between spending and revenue, sporting surpluses in only twelve of of sixty-eight years. The number of surplus years was smaller for the United States (9/68) compared to the United Kingdom (12/68), though the former's average of minus

2.2 percent was less negative than the latter's minus 2.6. A reader might think that the high incidence of deficits reflects an Anglo Saxon budgetary fecklessness compared, for example, with the prudent and frugal Germans.

Such is not the case. Despite a reputation for practicing strict rectitude in public finances, "balancing the budget" comes as recent custom for German governments. Statistics do not go back so far for other countries but still cover several decades. In only six of the twenty-three years between 1995 and 2017 did the reunited German government run a budget surplus; four of them come consecutively at the end, 2014–17, and two were in the previous nineteen years. For the other large countries of the European Union we find similar non-implementation of spending equal revenue. During the period 1995 to 2017, the French and Italian governments had no surplus years, and the Spanish government had just three. Moving to the medium-sized European countries, the only ones with a substantial number of surplus years during the twenty-three years 1995 to 2017 were Finland (11) and Sweden (12). Beyond North America and Europe, the government of Japan has overseen continuous deficits since 1992.

By demonstrating the relative rarity of "balancing the books," this brief survey of government budgets provides an operating definition of "fiscal austerity" or, more generally, "austerity policy." It also suggests why governments of large countries have not practiced it until recently. Austerity is not merely the exercise of cutting or limiting the growth of expenditure. Many circumstances occur during which a government may decide to cut expenditures (or raise taxes). An obvious case presents itself when economic expansion results in inflationary pressures. When that happens, policies to increase tax revenue or reduce expenditure may prove the most effective way to contain those inflationary pressures. Limiting expenditure or increasing taxes are policy responses of "demand management" by the government for the specific goal of reducing inflation.

After the global financial crisis of 2008, austerity came to mean a very specific public policy, the overriding goal of equating public expenditures to tax revenue. By "overriding," I mean that achieving a "balanced budget" took priority over all other economic and social policies. A balanced budget was the alleged precondition for economic recovery and stability, without which national welfare would suffer harm far greater than the temporary deprivation caused by expenditure reduction. For example, reductions in US federal expenditure on unemployment compensation would cause short-term suffering to many households but, by leading to a balanced budget, would rejuvenate the economy as a whole and bring down the number of people without work.

This programmatic framework found its selling rhetoric with the first famous and later infamous TINA principle: there is no alternative. A prominent invoking of this principle came with the prevention of widespread bankruptcies of financial corporations early in the global crisis of 2008–10. Several governments chose to prevent financial bankruptcies by recapitalizing the banks and other corporations, which were issued government bonds to replace assets rendered worthless by the financial crisis.

Financial corporations had made large volumes of high-risk loans, which the borrowers could not service

11

once the crisis hit North America and Europe. In several countries, notably the United Kingdom, the United States and Spain, recapitalization prevented the collapse of entire financial sectors. The bonds that rescued private finance meant that the savior governments increased their debts – to save banks and corporations, governments generated budget deficits and accumulated debt. The government of Spain provides a striking case. In 2008 the Spanish public debt stood at a modest 47 percent of GDP, well below that of the putatively prudent German government, at 67 percent. The Spanish public debt ratio rose to 78 percent in 2011 and to 106 percent in 2013, with almost all the additional debt accumulated to recapitalize the private financial sector (numbers from the EU online database "Eurostat"). The growth in public debt involved no spending increase on public services. Those bonds rested in private balance sheets as replacement assets for bad loans made before 2008.

By EU accounting rules, the issue of public bonds to private corporations counted as budgeted expenditures. Even though the Spanish government hardly increased its spending during the global crisis, the recapitalization of private finance resulted in a massive rise in the public-sector deficit. A budget surplus of 2 percent of GDP in 2007 became a deficit of 4.4 percent in 2008 with the first recapitalizations, then 11 percent in 2009, with an average of over 10 percent for the four years 2009–12.

These non-spending deficits created by recapitalization brought the Spanish government into conflict with the fiscal rules of the European Union. Those rules, subsequently made stricter, required corrective policies if public-sector deficits exceeded 3 percent of GDP and/ or public debt rose above 60 percent of GDP. As non-sensical as it was, the TINA principle dictated imposing austerity policies on the Spanish government. "There was no alternative" to bailing out the financial sector, otherwise the entire economy would have collapsed. After the bailout, "there was no alternative" to impos-ing budgetary austerity because the public-sector deficit soared to unacceptable levels as arbitrarily defined in EU treaties (the Treaty of Maastricht, later incorporated into the Treaty on European Union and the Treaty on the Functioning of the European Union).

An obvious alternative existed. In the early 1990s the Swedish financial sector faced imminent collapse. In response, the center-right government nationalized the banking sector, which involved no bailout (see "Sweden's Fix for Banks: Nationalize Them," *New York Times*, 22 January 2009). When the Swedish economy recovered, the government sold the nationalized banks back to private owners, realizing a profit on the sale. As a result, instead of the eponymous taxpayer funding a bailout, the public sector gained revenue via the bank "rescue."

If, unlike the policy of the Swedish government, a bailout results in a nominal deficit in the public budget, alternatives to expenditure cuts and/or tax increases come easily to mind. The most obvious would be to work with a cash-flow budget, in which case issuing bonds for recapitalization would not count into expenditure, since the recipient banks must hold them as assets. The more fundamental alternative to austerity budgeting would be to reduce the deficit to GDP ratio through economic expansion – i.e., increase the denominator (GDP) rather

13

than the numerator (the budget deficit). This policy approach features in our subsequent discussion.

A final comment is necessary on the TINA princi ple as applied to public debt. Bank recapitalisation in Spain, a free gift of safe assets to replace recklessly risky lending by private finance, was not without its element of black humor. Spanish private financial institutions used the recapitalization funds to speculate on Spanish government debt, which provoked a "sovereign debt" crisis by driving down bond values and inflating interest rates. To state it simply, the Spanish government saved the banks by giving them public bonds; and, returned to good health, the banks used their idle cash to specu- late on the bonds that had saved them from collapse. This scenario justifies a combination of the old clichés "biting the hand that feeds you" and "no good deed goes unpunished."

This excursion into the unstable quicksand of the TINA principle leads to a working definition of budg- etary austerity. As practiced across Europe and in the United States after the global crisis, the essential feature of austerity was to make a balanced budget the first pri- ority for government economic management, even to the point of enshrining it as a legal requirement. By its own design, after the global crisis the Spanish government created an austerity "perfect storm": an unprecedented recapitalization of banks resulted in unprecedented public deficits and debt under EU accounting rules; passage of a constitutional amendment requiring a bal- anced budget made the government legally bound to enforce draconian reductions in spending, during which time the banks that started it all enjoyed windfall profits on bond speculation.

## *Austerity in Practice*

We can now identify which governments have implemented austerity, in the specific sense of setting a balanced budget as their priority fiscal goal. Though seeking a balanced budget is the definition of austerity, success in achieving that goal is not a satisfactory indicator of implementing austerity. The gap between spending and revenue can widen or narrow for many reasons having little to do with government policy. To take an example, in a rapidly growing economy, tax income tends to rise faster than public expenditure because higher profits and wages mean households and corporations pay more. That can happen with no change in either public expenditure or tax rates.

Pro-austerity arguments tend to go along with the allegation that people do not want to pay more tax. If a government accepts or actively fosters that belief in tax phobia, austerity budgeting requires reducing expenditure. Figures 0.3 to 0.5 aid in the assessment of which governments did and which did not implement austerity. For those who find such charts tedious or daunting, I provide a full discussion that renders them optional.

When the global crisis began in 2008, the governments of both the United Kingdom and the United States responded with substantial expenditure increases whose purpose was to counteract the forces generating recession. In both countries, political events ended those expansionary budgets. In Britain, the election of May 2010 brought to government a center-right coalition explicitly committed to budget balancing. In the United States, the mid-term election of November 2010 created

*Figure 0.3 Index of total public expenditure, United Kingdom and United States, 2000–2017 (constant prices; year 2000 = 100)*

Note: In 2017 US federal government public expenditure was 18 percent of GDP; UK central government expenditure was 38 percent of GDP.

Source: US *Economic Report of the President 2018*; UK Office for National Statistics.

Republican majorities in both houses of Congress with legislative leaders committed to reducing public borrowing.

As figure 0.3 shows, in both countries for the first nine years of the new century public expenditure grew continuously. In 2010 austerity policies began, with inflation-adjusted expenditures falling in the United States and leveling off in the United Kingdom. In both cases a rapid reduction in public borrowing was the explicit goal. In the second half of the 2010s the new leadership of the British Labour Party pledged to end austerity budgeting should it come into government.

In the United States in 2017, with the arrival of the

16

presidency of Donald Trump, US budget policy changed. The Trump government showed no tendency to increase social expenditure. However, like the Reagan presidency in the 1980s and George W. Bush's administration in the 2000s, the Trump administration had no commitment to balancing budgets. To the contrary, it cut tax rates substantially, especially for those at the top of the distribution. As the Republican Party moved further to the right over four decades, it committed to balanced budgets when Democrats held the presidency, but abandoned that commitment when one of its own occupied the White House. Following that rather inconsistent approach to public spending and revenue, the Trump administration ended austerity budgeting in the strict sense of giving priority to "balancing the books."

Moving across the Atlantic, assessing the practice of austerity in the strict sense of budget balancing is straightforward for the countries of the European Union. In the mid-2010s, EU governments agreed to make balanced budgets – austerity – the central goal of public budgeting policy. The so-called Excessive Deficit Procedure of the Stability and Growth Pact committed all member governments to near-zero borrowing. Some governments, notably Spain's, enshrined this commitment in their national constitutions.

The four largest continental EU countries all had growing inflation-adjusted public expenditure in the years immediately before the global crisis (figure 0.4). Real expenditure declined dramatically in Spain after the global crisis. The sharp decline shows an unambiguous case of austerity policies. Over the same years expenditures fell in Italy, but considerably less in comparison with Spain. Nonetheless, the decline in expenditure

17

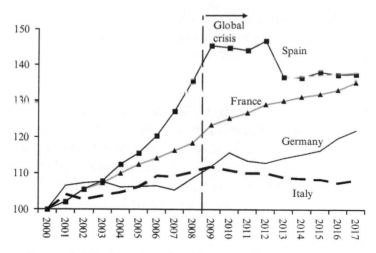

*Figure 0.4 Index of total public expenditure, four major eurozone countries, 2000–2017 (constant prices; year 2000 = 100)*

Source: Eurostat (statistical agency of the European Union).

by the Italian government was more than sufficient to qualify as an austerity policy. The implementation of expenditure cuts in both Italy and Spain followed from an explicit goal of eliminating deficits, and in both countries the austerity policy occurred as part of agreement with the European Commission.

In contrast, spending in real terms continued to expand in France and Germany after 2008. The explanation of why Italy and Spain implemented explicit deficit reduction policies while France and Germany did not lies in the politics among EU governments more than in the prudence, or lack of it, of the two governments.

Three smaller EU countries, Greece, Ireland and Portugal, implemented austerity programs of severe expenditure reduction. These three countries carry the dubious distinction of achieving fame, indeed infamy, as a result of budget programs imposed by external institutions, with the European Commission and the European Central Bank having the leading roles. In all three cases the imminent threat of collapse of national financial sectors led the governments to accept budget conditions devised by officials in the European Commission. Pressure from other EU governments, with the German government in the lead, left the governments of Greece, Ireland and Portugal with the stark choice of accepting extreme budget cuts or suffering national economic collapse.

The expenditure cuts were indeed severe (figure 0.5). In Greece, public expenditure reached its peak in 2011, 35 percent above that in 2000. Six years later, in 2017, inflation-adjusted expenditure had collapsed almost back to the level it had been in 2000. The Portuguese population suffered expenditure decline as extreme. From its peak in 2009, inflation-adjusted spending fell almost to the level of seventeen years before. Budget cuts were also violent in Ireland, whose rapid growth of spending up to 2007 came with budget surpluses, not deficits. The expansion of spending hit its peak in 2011 at more than double the 2000 level, then dropped rapidly over the next five years.

The important characteristic of the sharp drops in expenditure in the five EU countries was the conscious goal of achieving a budget in which revenue covered expenditure. By 2018 only the government of Greece had reached that goal. In the process of doing so, the national economy suffered the largest contraction of any in the European Union. In the chapters that follow I devote considerable analysis to that combination –

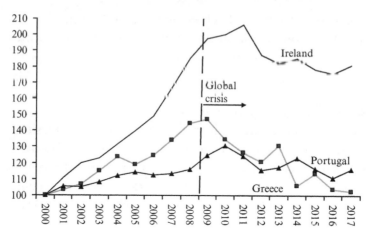

*Figure 0.5 Index of total public expenditure, three austerity-implementing eurozone countries, 2000–2017 (constant prices; year 2000 = 100)*

Source: Eurostat.

expenditure cuts achieving deficit reduction at the cost of economic contraction.

### Austerity Politics and Reality

The austerity-implementing EU governments were repeatedly confronted with the TINA argument by the institutions and governments funding their "bailouts." Unqualified, definitive judgments such as TINA-justified austerity policy frequently derive from abstract reasoning divorced from the nuances of concrete experience. These definitive policy judgments frequently emerge from carrying an otherwise reasonable hypothesis to its logical extreme.

Mainstream economics provides an example of such a

judgment. All economists share the insight that market economies possess self-adjustment mechanisms. To pursue that insight to the special case conclusion that adjustment quickly leads to full employment represents *reductio ad absurdum*. An otherwise valid insight, that market economies are characterized by relative stability, reaches an extreme conclusion that contradicts reality. The circle of improbability is squared by using the ideal outcome as the ruler to judge reality. In a triumph of logic over reality, the abstract principle treats as the problem the failure of reality to conform to the ideal.

Austerity policies involve a political choice. They do not come from imperatives of real-world economic conditions. They do not represent the accumulated wisdom of economic analysis and theory. The TINA principle does not apply to them. Austerity policies find their verisimilitude, the appearance of truth, in a series of interconnected myths, which the rest of this book deconstructs.

# 1

# We Must Live Within Our Means

### The Myth Itself

Perhaps the most difficult of all the austerity myths to pin down is the injunction that "we must live within our means." The message deeply embodied in this phrase has little relationship to the words. Rather, it serves as the apparently definitive answer to the question "Can our government spend more?" We can imagine a politician speaking at a meeting of constituents, and a concerned citizen asks, "Why is it necessary to reduce spending on school meals?" And the elected representative answers, "The overall government budget is in deficit and we must live within our means."

If the constituent retorted with, "Why must we live within our means?," the assembled group might break into laughter, because every sensible person knows "we must live within our means." If the constituent instead went to the heart of the matter and asked, "What do you mean by 'means'?," the politician, if a patient person, might say, "I mean that the government obtains its money from taxation and we cannot spend money we do not have." That would probably induce affirmative nods from the audience.

What are our "means" and what or who determines them? What does "live within" convey? A dictionary provides no enlightenment. Equally vacuous is the closely related phrase, often applied to household budgets, that "families struggle to make ends meet." These clichés serve as emotional entreaties rather than practical guidelines, like "emojis" at the end of an email.

When in the 1980s the UK Prime Minister Margaret Thatcher made her famous assertion that government budgets are like household budgets, she was half right for the wrong reason. She was wrong in that, unlike her mythical households, real households do not operate with balanced budgets. They borrow long-term to invest (mortgages) and short-term to bridge temporary financial difficulties (such as when changing jobs and when faced with emergency expenditures). Governments do the same: they borrow to invest (e.g., in schools and hospitals) and to cover short-term emergencies (recessions).

To understand how this happens and its full implications, we must specify some concrete circumstances. The clearest way to begin the discussion is to analyze central governments in countries that have their own national currencies – the US dollar, British pound, Japanese yen and Chinese renminbi are the most important ones by size of the transactions they facilitate. Central governments with national currencies have "central banks" (e.g., the Bank of England and the US Federal Reserve System), public institutions that manage the national currency within the constraints of the legal mandate set by the central government itself.

23

To be even more concrete, we begin with governments in high-income countries that have their own currencies. This specification is necessary because financial markets in low-income countries and in many middle-income countries (sometimes identified as "emerging economies") have unsophisticated financial sectors of relatively low development. Many central banks operate through financial markets, but small or undeveloped financial markets in which a few banks or corporations have disproportionate power severely limit the ability of central banks to conduct policy.

The discussion that follows applies to North America (Canada and the United States), the Western European countries with national currencies (the United Kingdom, Denmark, Norway, Sweden and Switzerland), Japan and some of the middle income countries of Asia, but almost no African country except South Africa. An important caveat is necessary. The rules on central government borrowing and central bank operations vary across countries. Our discussion and analysis apply most closely to the UK and the US, whose government institutions are quite similar when considering the relationship between the central government and the central bank.

The fundamental difference is that a government of a country with its own currency can borrow from itself, which households cannot. To use a cliché, the ability of a government to borrow from itself is a "game changer." Governments with their own currencies can always "make ends meet," though they must be wise in managing their "means." It is not a simple task. Explaining how governments and central banks pull off this apparent trick – making ends meet that are

24

unmeetable for households – takes center place in our first myth-busting.

## What Are Our Means?

Central to the austerity narrative is the apparently innocuous advice that we should "live within our means," a rule for sound household money management. For households, by "living within our means," we "make ends meet." For governments, this bit of common sense means not spending "what isn't there" and always being sure "where the money will come from." We find the same semi-moral entreaty applied to entire countries. If what we import and consume from other countries exceeds our exports, then we go into debt with other countries to cover the difference. As a country, we "live beyond our means" and "need to tighten our belts."

Moving from clichés to real-world practice, households, businesses, governments and countries need not and frequently do not live within their means. When they do not, they incur "debt." Further along we analyze the nature of debt and the forms it takes. In anticipation of that analytical discussion, I define debt tautologically as the result of not living within our means, not making ends meet.

"Living within our means" has a superficial validity that brings to mind George Joye's definition in 1535 of common sense as "the plain wisdom that everyone possesses." About 400 years later the American social theorist Stuart Chase commented, "common sense tells us the world is flat." Treating the world as flat is not necessarily absurd. It can be both rational and necessary. For many tasks, such as driving an automobile from one city to another, the flat-earth hypothesis works. It's just common sense that a straight road is the shortest distance between home and the supermarket. But no airline pilot or ship's navigator should adopt it. The common-sense flat-earth hypothesis applies as far as the horizon (myopically), but not much beyond. For substantial distances navigators use what is known as the "Great Circle Route," the shortest distance between two points on a globe (the orthodromic route). By analogy, the common-sense understanding of "means" as a flow of income has limited relevance beyond the horizon of the household.

In practice a household funds its expenditures in three ways – the incomes received by its members (from work, income-generating assets such as stocks and bonds, or social support payments from governments), the sale of assets, or borrowing. Most people in Europe and North America work for someone else. The regularly employed receive incomes determined by a contract with the employer. This contractual arrangement provides the greatest part of their "means." Rational budgeting for the regularly employed treats income, the means, as fixed by the employer, household asset values and government support programs.

In these circumstances, "living within our means" has a clear interpretation. The sum of household expenditures over the budget period should be equal to or less than the fixed and predictable income flow during that time period. The household manager has little control over the determinants of income but can purchase less or more. Introductory economics textbooks describe "making ends meet" as the household operating "within a budget constraint." The phrases are equivalent.

If variable expenditures exceed fixed income, the household must either sell assets or borrow. Sale of assets means a fall in household wealth. Only a few households, the very rich, can continue this indefinitely (which provides support for Hemingway's famous retort to F. Scott Fitzgerald when he said: "Ernest, the rich are different from us"; Hemingway replied, "Yes, they have more money"). The other option, we "live beyond our means" funded by borrowing, results in a debt that the household must finance out of its fixed income flow.

From the household point of view, failing to cover expenditure with the flow of income results in what are clearly undesirable outcomes. Household wealth declines either directly, by sales of assets, or indirectly, by going into debt that reduces net wealth (household assets minus liabilities). In addition, the running cost of not living within your means increases by the interest on the accumulating debt. Borrowing provides a temporary solution, but the cost of servicing the accumulating debt increases the difficulty of "making ends meet."

In practice the cost of borrowing tends to vary inversely with income. The lower a household is on the income pyramid, the higher is the interest rate to borrow because lenders consider the poor risky clients. This empirical generalization, "the poor pay more," in part explains the infamous "sub-prime" mortgage market in the United States, whose collapse provided the trigger (but not the cause) for the global financial crisis of the late 2000s.

Some household borrowing creates assets, such as mortgages for a home and loans to purchase an automobile. If properly evaluated, these debts should prove expenditure-reducing rather than expenditure-increasing for households. This type of borrowing creates an asset to balance against the debt. The interest payments on the asset-creating loan become part of the expenditure that household income must cover. The asset "pays for itself" because it generates a service that replaces part of household spending (e.g., mortgage cost replaces rent).

These one-off borrowings do not contradict the myopic generalization that a household should live within its means. The perspective of the precariously employed and the rich will be quite different. But the middle-class perspective, that of Margaret Thatcher, holds tightly to the sound budgeting parable, that households must constrain their variable expenditures within the fixed income flow, in order to keep "living within their means."

The flat-earth approach to budgeting does not apply to governments, local or national, whose incomes (their "means") are not fixed. "Means" are a political choice. The power to tax gives the power to determine the "means" within which a government operates. For that reason alone we can dismiss the simple myth that "governments have only so much income and must live within it." Governments determine their means by establishing and modifying the tax structure and rates, subject to accountability to the electorate. The more sophisticated version of the parable is that, whatever income governments choose to generate by tax, they must live within it – i.e., they must balance their budgets.

# We Must Live Within Our Means

## *How Governments Borrow*

Before deconstructing the government balancing act (the second myth), we must complete the analysis of what determines the means within which governments should operate. "Means" of a government are not the same as tax revenue. As for households, governments can borrow. The outcome of government borrowing is different than it is for households. The first step to analyze public-sector borrowing is to be explicit about the process. Bonds – promises to pay – provide the mechanism for public borrowing at all levels of government.

A bond is a piece of paper (even in this digital age) that commits the borrower both to pay the purchaser (lender) a specific amount by a stated future date and to pay interest on the specified amount. For example, a local or national government might offer for sale a $100 (or £100 or €100) bond that promises full repayment a year later (the "maturity date"), and during that year to pay 5 percent of the sale price to the buyer for the privilege of having the buyer's money for that twelve months.

Buyers of government bonds may be businesses, commercial banks, households, public institutions, or other governments. For all buyers, public bonds function as an extremely important, irreplaceable asset. Except under unusual circumstances (treated in Myth 2), public bonds represent an extremely safe asset. In 2018 the private companies that rate corporate and public bonds assigned the "debt paper" of Britain, France, Germany and the United States to their safest category ("AAA"). The bonds of the British government are frequently

29

known as "gilts," because in the past the paper on which they were printed was literally gilt-edged.

Public bonds themselves are a "liquid" (vendible) asset. Should the holder of a public bond want cash before the end of the bond's life, the owner can sell that bond to anyone willing to purchase it. By convention these resales are said to occur in a "secondary market." In secondary markets public bonds may encounter speculation, a possibility considered later in the discussion of the function of public debts. At this point we focus on the dual nature of public bonds, a liability for the issuing government (a debt to be repaid) and a safe asset for the purchaser.

The next step is to consider borrowing for different levels and types of governments. In many countries, local and state (or provincial) governments can and do borrow, usually to finance investment projects such as public transport. In 2010 the outstanding stock of bonds issued by US municipal governments reached almost $4 trillion, almost all of which held AAA investment rating. Analogously to household borrowing, sub-national governments cover the interest and repayment (the "debt service") by tax revenue ("general obligation" bonds) or the income generated by the investment project itself (e.g., public transport charges). All over the world, and especially in North America and Europe, sub-national governments "live within their means" by taxing and borrowing.

The myopic common-sense view that governments, like households, "should not spend money that isn't there" turns out to be more nuanced that it first appears. By selling bonds, sub-national governments transfer money from the private sector to themselves. As a result, governments have more money "there" to spend. For the economy as a whole this money transfer involves a shift of private saving to public spending.

Sub-national governments can extend the horizon of their "means." National governments can completely discard the flat-earth approach to budgets. When considering the budgeting of national governments we must go straight to the Great Circle approach and leave the common-sense funding horizon behind. Separating national governments into two categories is the next step to understand the meaning of how they "live within their means." The two categories are governments of countries with a national currency (US dollar, British pound, Japanese yen) and those countries that share a common currency. The eurozone is the most important shared currency group, distantly followed by the fourteen-member common currency zone in French-speaking sub-Saharan Africa (all using the so-called CFA franc). Because of the extremely low development of the financial sectors of CFA countries, they are not relevant to our discussion.

For public budgets, the most important consequence of a country possessing its own currency is that the national government – but not sub-national governments – can borrow from itself. The process begins in the same way it did with the sub-national governments. The national government sets out its expenditure plans to meet its commitments to its citizens. If these expenditures exceed the flow of public revenue, the government "makes ends meet" by borrowing – selling the private sector its bonds. The national government has an option not available to a sub-national government (much less households and corporations), which permits Great Circle finance – it can sell its bonds to itself.

The formal process involves an intra-government exchange between the department in charge of budgeting ("treasury") and the institution responsible for management of the currency ("central bank"). In the United States these are the Department of the Treasury and the Federal Reserve Bank; in Britain, they are Her Majesty's Treasury and the Bank of England. The government (the executive) instructs the treasury to sell bonds to the central bank. The central bank, which is the government's banker, pays for the bonds by creating credit for the government equal to the face value of the new bond issue.

This exchange, where the government receives credit and the central bank receives bonds, has a technical name: "monetizing the deficit." A more correct name would be "monetized borrowing." The word "monetization" indicates that the bond sale has generated an amount of money (in the form of central bank credit) equal to the value of the bond sale. When bonds are sold to a household, a corporation or even a government agency other than the central bank, we have what might be named "de-monetized borrowing." Consider the simple case in which a person buys a US bond with cash. The private economy then has less cash in circulation by the amount the person paid for the bond. When the central bank buys the government bond, private cash holdings do not change.

In both cases the government's purpose in borrowing would be to fund expenditure. Selling a $100 (£100 or €100) bond to any buyer other than the central bank increases expenditure (by 100) and leaves money in

32

private circulation unchanged (100 comes out of the private economy when the bond is bought, then 100 goes into the private economy when the government expenditure is made). A simple example of non-monetization: a retired woman receives a weekly pension of $100 on Monday; on Tuesday she purchases a $100 government bond, and her net cash flow for the two days is zero. On the Monday of the same week the government sells a $100 bond to the central bank and the central bank credits $100 to a government checking account; on Tuesday the government uses the $100 credit to purchase memory sticks from a computer shop; money in the private sector increases by $100.

These simple examples demonstrate how the national government of a country with its own currency always "lives within its means." The government can expand its means by borrowing from itself. The governments of Canada, Japan, the United Kingdom and the United States can never "run out of money." The money "is always there." Before turning to the spectre lurking in the background – inflation – two important implications need stating. Governments of countries with national currencies 1) can never default on their debt ("go bankrupt") and 2) need never suffer from speculation that drives up interest rates on their bonds.

The first is easily understood. If a government can borrow from itself, it has the option of buying back the bonds held in the private economy by selling bonds to the central bank: when 1 billion of privately held bonds reaches maturity date, the government that issued the bonds sells 1 billion new bonds to the central bank and uses the central bank credit to pay private bond holders. Only as a political choice would a government with a national currency default on – rather than repurchase – its debt.

How does a government with its own currency prevent speculation on its bonds? During 2010–15, several governments of eurozone countries suffered from speculative runs on their public bonds. To take the most notorious example, in early 2010 the Greek government sold its bonds at an interest rate of 5 percent. Two years later those same bonds carried an interest rate of almost 40 percent. This extraordinary increase resulted from a speculative attack facilitated by European Union treaties that limit the possible actions of the European Central Bank. Holders of Greek bonds, almost certainly acting in collusion, began to sell – dump – their bonds, which drove the sale price well below the face value; a €100 bond issued in early 2010 at 5 percent yielded almost 40 percent on the secondary (resale) market, a collapse in the bond price from €100 to €12.50.

Such a massive fall is an embarrassment producing a disaster. In order to borrow more, the Greek government needed to issue a new €100 bond at an annual interest rate of 40 percent. No private buyer would accept less because of the availability of older bonds at speculation-depressed prices.

This appalling scenario need never happen in a country with a national currency. Suppose the British government wanted to raise £10 billion through a bond sale at 2 percent annual interest. If the bonds cannot be sold to private buyers at that interest rate, the government sells to the Bank of England. Speculative attacks on British, American, Japanese and other national currency bonds occur only if the government allows it. They need not happen.

## We Must Live Within Our Means

Why do governments with national currencies ever sell their bonds in the private sector? Why owe it to others when we can owe it to ourselves? This apparently perplexing question has a straightforward answer – sale of public bonds to the private economy serves extremely important policy functions. When a government sells bonds to the private sector it reduces the total credit or money of the private sector. When it buys bonds the government increases credit and money. Bond sales and purchases, "open market operations" by a central bank (the abbreviation OMO is commonly used), are a mechanism to increase or decrease money in circulation (though controversy rages over the effectiveness of doing so).

Conventional wisdom maintains that sales and purchases of bonds provide an important policy instrument for central banks to moderate inflationary pressures or stimulate spending (though the former is believed to be more effective than the latter). Whether OMO provide an effective mechanism is a source of considerable controversy among academic economists. This debate, extremely important for understanding monetary policy, can be briefly summarized.

The bonds issued by governments with national currencies should not be viewed merely as debt (a liability). These bonds play a major role as a policy tool of central banks. Instability and cycles of "boom and bust" plague market economies and have done so for two hundred years. It would seem a reasonable presumption that central banks might moderate this instability by reducing and increasing the amount of money in the private economy.

We would expect that reducing money in circulation

35

would impact on how much households and businesses spend. In response to less private expenditure we would expect businesses to produce less. Therefore, if policy makers believe that production and employment are so strong that undesirable inflationary pressures are imminent, they would seek to reduce money in circulation. If recession is expected, policy makers would take steps to increase the amount of money in circulation. To reduce money in circulation, the central bank would sell government securities to banks. With fewer money assets on their balance sheets, the capacity of banks to extend credit contracts. Central bank purchases of bonds should have the opposite effect, increasing bank cash holdings and thus the capacity to lend.

Simply put, the sale of bonds would make money scarcer, causing interest rates to rise, which should discourage private investment. Buying bonds would make money more abundant, which should stimulate investment.

The goal of these "open market operations" is to manage the quantity of money in the private economy. In the late 1980s the world's major central banks abandoned this approach because financial deregulation appeared to make OMO ineffective. In their place central banks began to set interest rates directly. While this shift to setting interest rates did not make OMO irrelevant, it demoted them to a supportive role in central bank policy.

Direct setting of interest rates has made the heads of central banks into major public figures. Rumors of rate changes provoke speculation in the media with the explicit message that the usually quite small adjustments in interest rates will have substantial impact on the economy. There is controversy among economists (and policy makers) over the analysis that justifies the links between interest rates, on the one hand, and economic activity, on the other. An influential minority of the economics profession argues that the links have little empirical evidence to support them, and the actions by central banks have limited impact on national economies.

At the heart of the controversy over the impact of OMO and direct interest-rate adjustments lies an easily understood analytical issue, what can serve as money? In practice a myriad of things function as money for transactions. Governments have quite limited control over the quantity of money as means of circulation and certainly do not hold a "money monopoly." Fewer things can function to settle debts, and fewer still as a store of value that protects against inflationary periods and depressions. To take a simple example, a person can purchase a used lawn mower from a neighbor with an IOU for $150. However, at some point the IOU must be paid off with cash (which is a US government-backed IOU). The IOU functioned as money as the medium of exchange but cannot serve to settle the debt. For OMO and direct interest-rate adjustments to be effective, policy makers must know and verify in the real world the links between the different forms of money and also non-money that for some purposes can serve as money.

The sales of public bonds and/or the central bank raising the interest rate on those bonds may well increase the rate banks charge to businesses seeking to borrow and invest. However, like the person who bought a lawn mower with an IOU, it is open to those businesses to finance their investments by sale or trade of stocks or their own bonds. As a result, the practical impact of central bank actions on businesses' investment may be negligible.

While financial instability has many causes, the various functions of money can play a major role provoking them. In buoyant times businesses have a tendency to build up substantial IOU debt in the form of their own "junk bonds" or "supplier credits" (contractual deferred payment). The sales income of businesses provides the confidence that the business IOUs will be settled with cash. Should a recession hit, debtors can discover that they no longer have the cash flow to clear their debts, provoking a widespread collapse of debt value.

In this context, open market operations should not be confused with so-called quantitative easing (QE). QE is a one-way street – purchase of assets, bonds or stocks from corporations and commercial banks. Governments carried out these purchases to prevent corporate bankruptcy, earning the derogatory moniker "bailouts." Whether the bailouts, which transferred cash to corporations, had a positive impact on the aggregate economy of the countries in which they occurred is even more controversial than the effectiveness of open market operations.

Another important difference between OMO and QE is that the former are literally "open." Both the buying and the selling of government bonds by the central bank occur fully in the public eye through financial market transactions. In contrast, quantitative easing involves purchases (never sales) by a central bank of assets of financial and non-financial corporations. Government bonds are auctioned on pre-announced dates in the United States through the public agency Treasury Direct and in Britain by the government's Debt Management

Office. Quantitative easing operations are quite different. The central bank identifies specific items for purchase (public bonds, private debt or other assets). Why the central bank chooses a specific corporation for these purchases is not always clear.

Every debt (liability) is someone's asset. Household debt for a mortgage is an asset for the bank that made the loan. Business debt, usually incurred to make an investment, is an asset for the lender. In addition to going into debt for homes, many people save – for example, to fund children's education or for retirement. When people do this, they need a safe way to protect that saving. Businesses accumulate cash through their commercial activities. The frequent time gaps between sales and expenditures may leave businesses with idle cash, temporary idle balances.

Household and business savings lead directly to a second important function of public borrowing, as store of value. Public bonds provide the private sector with a safe asset, for households, commercial banks and other corporations. In recent years, private bond holders in Britain, the United States and Germany have complained of a shortage of public bonds –not enough public debt!

It may seem strange that households and business would willingly put their savings into assets (public bonds) that in the 2010s paid almost zero interest. Why would a corporation or a person lend the government money at no charge? A moment of reflection shows that such behavior is quite understandable. The vast majority of households seek a safe form in which to hold their unspent income (if they have any). The payment of interest represents icing on the cake of financial security. In ancient times through to the Middle Ages, wealth holders paid merchants a fee for keeping their assets safe from thieves. Public bonds serve a similar function.

In most years the demand for public bonds is strong in all developed countries with national currencies. Except under unusual circumstances the governments of these countries, in North America, Europe and Asia, have no difficulty selling their bonds at low interest rates. A clear case of "usual circumstances" occurred in some of the eurozone countries, circumstances that result from these governments not having national currencies. These circumstances come up for inspection under Myth 4, "Never go into debt."

### Public Sector Auto-Finance

In 1967 Fred Hoyle, the UK Astronomer Royal and world-famous cosmologist, published a short story in which a meteor of solid gold strikes ground in Britain (found in the collection titled, appropriately enough, *Element 79*). Were this landfall to occur, among the many implications (all leading to disaster in the story) is that the government would suddenly find that, for all practical purposes, it had no limit to its ability to spend. After securing the meteor site as a public monopoly, whenever a government bill comes due a Treasury official would chip off a bit of gold and use it as payment.

Entertaining as the short story is (and I recommend it), the premise barely qualifies as fiction. In practice a government with a national currency has a more effective limitless spending source than a gold meteor. That source is the ability to borrow from itself – "auto-finance." Its implications can now be pursued further. As explained above, in this process the government receives an amount of credit that it spends (the motivation for the borrowing). This spending injects an amount of money into the hands of businesses or people equal to the amount the government borrowed from the central bank. This injection might occur through payment of civil service salaries or purchase of specific goods and services (such as payment to a construction company for repairing a bridge). The borrowing itself increases the government's deficit.

Even when demand for bonds is strong in financial markets and the government could easily sell its bonds to private buyers, there are compelling arguments for keeping sales within the public sector – selling bonds to the central bank or some other public institution. Stimulating the economy is the first and most obvious reason for monetization. If the economy has idle resources, the increased spending will provoke business to produce more, which requires bringing some of those idle resources into use.

Were the increased spending funded by increased taxes rather than borrowing, the stimulating effect would be far less. What the increased spending puts into the economy the increased tax revenue would take out, though not completely, as I explain below. If the increased spending were funded by increased borrowing in financial markets, the spending injection would be accompanied by a reduction in money held by businesses and households. That reduction in money in circulation might have a contractionary effect on the economy. Monetizing the borrowing – selling bonds to the central bank – would give the biggest "bang for the

41

buck" in a spending package. It would increase spending and increase money in circulation in the private sector.

Funding expenditure by taxation brings to mind the common generalization that "all is not what it seems." This applies to government spending and taxation as much or more than it does to politics. It might appear that, if a government spends $100 and covers that spending by a tax increase of $100, the net effect on the economy is zero – $100 into the economy, $100 out ($100 – $100 = 0). As obvious as it may appear, that conclusion is not valid. A step-by-step deconstruction reveals the fallacy.

Step 1: The government increases its tax revenue by $100 from households.

Step 2: If the government had not increased taxes, households would have spent most of the $100 and not spent (saved) a small portion. In the UK and the US the average household saving rate in 2018 was about 5 percent; in Germany it was 10 percent and in Japan 20 percent.

Step 3: When the governments in the UK and the US tax £/$100 from households, private spending falls by £/$95; in Germany it falls by €90 and in Japan by ¥80.

Step 4: When the government increases its spending by 100, the initial effect in the UK and the US is +5; in Germany it is +10 and in Japan +20.

To summarize, when a government increases taxes and spending by the same amount, the result is a net increase in total spending, because part of what government has taxed households and businesses would not have been spent.

42

## We Must Live Within Our Means

If this result comes as unexpected, it becomes stranger still. The saving rate by households and businesses has no impact on the expansionary effect of increasing tax and expenditure by the same amount. The net expansionary effect is always equal to the increase in spending. This unexpected outcome results because the same saving rate applies to both the increase in spending (where it has an expanding effect) and the increase in taxes (where it has a contracting effect). Whatever the saving rate in the economy, a simultaneous increase in expenditure and tax of (for example) $1 billion expands the economy by $1 billion. This general point explains why increases in expenditure are more effective in stimulating the economy than decreases in tax. Households and businesses will save part of a tax decrease while the government spends all of a spending increase.

A second and perhaps less obvious motivation for monetization of borrowing is its distributional impact. The wealthier portion of the population buys government bonds. General taxation funds the interest on the bonds. Because the average taxpayer tends to have an income lower than the average bond holder, the effect of selling bonds to the private sector is to increase income inequality. The result is a transfer of income from the average taxpayer to the average bond holder. The importance of this effect varies by country. If the income tax system is highly progressive – tax rates rise sharply with income – the net distribution effect will be small because the income of the average taxpayer and the average bond holder will be close together.

Foreign purchases are a third reason not to sell government bonds in financial markets. Concerns about undue influence by foreign governments holding another government's bonds involve a political judgment specific to each country and moment. Foreign creditors, even governments, have an interest in keeping strong the currency of the debt they hold, implying that these creditors would avoid a sudden mass selling of public debt except under extreme circumstances.

A more concrete consequence of selling bonds abroad is the income flow effect. If residents hold all public debt, a closed taxation–interest circle results; what the government takes in tax from residents to pay interest it returns to residents (though not to the same residents). By contrast, interest paid on public debt held abroad causes a net outflow. This outflow is like an export not matched by an import. A resident produces a good or service to earn the income from which the tax comes to fund the interest transferred abroad. The result is a net outflow of real resources.

Foreigners, mostly foreign governments, held about one-third of the US public debt and about one-fourth of the British public debt in the mid-2010s. One-third and one-fourth of total interest payments amount to a small but not negligible share of national income, 0.9 and 0.6 percent, respectively. Some countries at specific times have suffered severely from the outflow of interest payments. Selling bonds to the central bank – the government borrowing from itself – avoids this financial outflow.

To summarize the effect of foreign ownership of public debt, recall that every debt is someone else's asset; for each borrower there is a lender. When debtor and creditor reside in the same country, the servicing of debt involves a financial transfer that has no direct impact on national production or income. The most important policy concern about intra-country transfers is distributional effects, because the average income of creditors is typically greater than that for debtors.

The creditor residing abroad creates the possibility of negative economic effects on the economy as a whole. While for most countries the effect is minor, a simple calculation indicates how negative effects might arise. Let the value of an economy's production of goods and services be 100 units (dollars, pounds, euros, etc.). That production of 100 generates incomes of the same amount (wages and profits). Assume that the interest on public and private debts of the country paid to non-residents is 5 units. Exports of 5 units are required to pay the interest owed to non-residents.

The income of the domestic employees and employers producing the goods and services remains 100, but the goods and services they can buy has fallen to 95. The demand for goods and services exceeds the supply. The excess demand ($100 - 95 = 5$) is satisfied by imports or provokes inflation. An inflow of imports unmatched by export revenue (which goes to non-residents as debt service) implies an increase in public or private foreign debt, which may make the excess demand problem worse.

Inflationary pressures result if the government seeks to stop the growth of debt owed to non-residents by limiting imports. If debt service is a substantial portion of national income, the inflationary pressures can prove quite severe. In Latin America in the 1980s and into the 1990s, external debt service rose to over 10 percent of national income in several countries, provoking high inflation rates (numbers from the World Bank's *Development Indicators*). For example, debt service (interest plus principle) rose above 10 percent of national income for the governments of Argentina (2003), Brazil (1999) and Mexico (1986 and 1996); this was also the situation for the Turkish government (2002).

A few eurozone countries experienced levels of debt service outflows well above 10 percent of national income as late as 2017, most notably Greece, Ireland and Portugal (European Central Bank, *Statistical Warehouse*). The residents of these countries were in effect sending abroad over 1 out of every 10 euros they earned. Their governments avoided inflationary pressures by applying severe austerity measures, tax increases and expenditure cuts, and the resulting fiscal surpluses eliminated the excess demand caused by debt service. The European Commission had a major role in design of these austerity packages, which generated considerable criticism across Europe.

Borrowing from oneself is not an option open to households or businesses. In whatever form or by whatever complicated instrument they contract their debts, these debts at some point encounter the necessity for cancellation by "cold hard cash." If anyone doubted this, and some did, the global financial crisis at the end of the 2000s demonstrated unambiguously the function of government-guaranteed money as the necessary debt-cancellation instrument.

The countries that are members of the eurozone represent a hybrid case that makes the importance of a national currency clear. The countries of the eurozone all have national central banks. In principle these central banks could extend credit to the governments of the country in euros. Had those central banks done so during and after the global financial crisis, the "sovereign debt" crisis of the eurozone countries would not have occurred. Like the US Federal Reserve, the Bank of Japan or the Bank of England, a eurozone national central bank could have prevented bond speculation by lending to its government at a low interest rate. For example, in 2011, the expenditures of the Greek government exceeded its revenue, requiring it to borrow. Had it borrowed from the Bank of Greece it could have done so at an interest rate chosen by the government. In doing so, the Bank of Greece would have created more euros, crediting them to an account of the Greek Finance Ministry.

This was not done in Greece or any other eurozone country because, by EU treaty, only the European Central Bank (ECB) has the authority to increase or decrease the supply of euros. The ECB itself could have purchased national bonds and thus prevented the eurozone debt crisis. For political reasons it did not do so, the discussion of which goes beyond the scope of this book.

No such restriction need constrain central banks in countries with national currencies. Some legislatures have created binding legal limits to the government borrowing from its central bank, though not in any major country. As a result, governments of countries with national currencies need never "run out of money," "fail to make ends meet," or "go bankrupt." Auto-borrowing does have its limits and should be done with a clear policy purpose in full consideration of those limits. Those limits are explained under Myth 4, "Never go into debt."

A final caveat is necessary to clarify how and why

governments with their own currencies borrow from themselves. A government borrows from itself by selling a bond to its central bank. Why bother with selling a bond for, say, $1,000? If the government owns the central bank – the case in almost every country with its own currency – why not bypass the bond and instruct the central bank to create in a government account an additional $1,000?

This suggestion has a simple answer. Like most *reductio ad absurdum* arguments, it fails to appreciate the purpose of the more complex process, in this case bond sales. Bond sales provide a sensible and prudent method of financing deficits, while direct transfers from the central bank to its government are fecklessly irresponsible. The difference arises because of the uncertain nature of economic policy making.

Policy makers can estimate the likely outcome of their actions, but actual outcomes are affected by many influences over which governments have no control. Consider the circumstance in which the economy is stagnating at an unacceptably high level of unemployment. To stimulate demand in order to prompt stronger private-sector growth, the government increases public expenditure by an increase in the pay of public-sector workers. Deficit finance via bond sales to the central bank funds the increased expenditure.

Soon after implementing the expenditure, policy makers discover that their expansion of demand successfully simulates employment but generates unexpected and undesirable inflationary pressure. However, the government cannot reverse the pay increase, which is in process. The bond sale mechanism provides the instrument to contain inflation while maintaining the fiscal expansion. Where previously it sold bonds and spent the funds from the sale, now it sells more bonds but does not spend, instead extracting cash from the private sector and hoarding it in the central bank. Bond sales provide both the financing vehicle for the additional expenditure and the instrument to stop inflationary pressure should it appear.

If the funding for the increased expenditure came from direct credit to the government from the central bank, policy makers would lack an effective tool to stop any unexpected inflationary pressure. They would have to choose between reducing government-generated demand by cutting public expenditure or raising tax rates, both of which involve delays before they have their desired effect. In addition, reducing money in the private sector through bond sales would be considerably less politically controversial than expenditure cuts or increases in tax rates. The buying and selling of bonds provides the mechanism for governments to escape from spending policies that generate unforeseen results. Wise governments plan for unexpected outcomes and create mechanisms to respond to them.

A more general point lurks below the surface. Rational governments use fiscal policy – spending and taxation – and the open market operations of monetary policy to complement each other. The buying and selling of government bonds is the mechanism that creates this complementarity.

## *From Myth to Reality*

For a household, income appears fixed and expenditure seems discretionary. It follows that spending must be squeezed within the limits of income, that people "must live within their means." In contrast, for a government of a country with a national currency, the "means" are discretionary, both through adjusting tax rates to alter revenue flow and by borrowing. These two discretionary policy tools, adjusting tax rates and the ability to borrow, imply that tax revenue (government income) does not constrain the expenditure policies of national governments.

The simplistic view that tax functions as a binding constraint on government expenditure is false. It is a myth. We find this fallacy used to justify major policy conclusions by those who oppose a greater role for the government. For example, we frequently encounter the argument that, while our government could raise taxes in order to spend more, most people if not all oppose higher taxes. Yes, our government could in theory tax us more to cover more spending, but we can rule that out as politically untenable.

This is a thinly veiled repeat of the "living within our means" myth. Whether or not voters in general oppose tax increases is a matter of opinion. In all countries great diversity characterizes the voting population. Differences in class, income, ethnicity and age may translate into differences in political views. But, even if it were the case that voters hold an unwavering opposition to tax increases, increased public revenue is not a necessary condition for increased public spending.

We Must Live Within Our Means

Another common and slightly more sophisticated variation of the "living within our means" myth is that, while we can borrow, this borrowing creates a debt that must be repaid. Therefore, borrowing to fund public services is an illusion that we can live within our means when in practice we cannot. Borrowing merely shifts the day of tax reckoning to the future. The burden of paying for the services we enjoy today will fall on generations to come.

Subsequent discussion deconstructs this and other myths. As we plow on, it is important that we do not let the "living within our means" myth creep back into our thinking in other guises. "Living within our means" has no relevance for governments of countries with national currencies. By holding tightly to that revelation, the other myths are revealed as false guides.

# 2

# Governments Must Balance Their Books

### *The Myth Itself*

The dispelling of our first austerity myth, "living within our means," established that the government in a country with its own currency need not equate tax revenue with expenditure. It need not "balance its budget." What is possible is not necessarily wise. Is borrowing sound policy? In practice, governments do not have to "balance their books," but should they?

Behavioral guidelines rarely come with per se justifications ("just do it!"). When rain is predicted, friends or family members advise us to carry an umbrella. They offer this advice to avoid us being soaked in a downpour, which is undesirable in itself and could possibly lead to an unpleasant malady such as the common cold. If the recipient of the advice retorts, "The forecast has changed and now predicts no rain," the umbrella warning would be withdrawn.

Operating with this sensible principle, one should ask why it is wise for a government to balance its books.

# Governments Must Balance Their Books

The justifications offered for "balancing the books" cite maladies that allegedly result directly from public borrowing. The two most frequently encountered are 1) the danger of deficits accumulating into a debilitating debt burden and 2) fears that deficits provoke inflation. The analysis of the fourth myth, "Never go into debt," inspects the first of these, and discussion of possible inflationary effects comes towards the end of the book.

The "balance the books" cliché subsumes several issues about budgets rarely made explicit. To take two obvious ones: what should be balanced, and over what time period? Conventional answers to these questions are that total revenue should equal total spending and that balancing should be an annual goal. Both answers are arbitrary, with little or no analytical or practical justification. The next section pursues the question of what should be balanced. With regard to time span, most national governments have procedures organized around annual budgets, with these procedures set by long practice with no obvious technical basis.

The characteristics of spending and tax categories do not lend themselves to matching over a specific time period such as twelve months. While this does not in itself negate the putative imperative to balance the budget, it should leave one skeptical about assigning great importance to annual outcomes. Discussions of budget balancing (total revenue = total expenditure) over any time period typically treat expenditure and tax as undifferentiated amounts rather than as a combination of elements with various characteristics and different functions. To make further progress, we take apart ("disaggregate") both taxing and spending.

## *Budget Uncertainty*

Concern about whether governments should balance their books too often proceeds as if both tax and spending were totals that governments can accurately plan and achieve. The presumption that governments control spending and tax outcomes leads to the expectation that the balance between the two, the surplus or deficit, is also well within the power of governments to control. With this presumption of predictability and control, the media frequently take politicians to task for "not meeting their targets," especially targets for deficit reduction.

In practice, total spending, total tax revenue and the balance between them are uncertain outcomes over which the taxing and spending government has less than full control. The root cause of the lack of control is the interactive nature of what the government does and the response of the economy, and vice versa. As developed in greater detail below, government tax and spending policies affect the ebb and flow of private economic activity; and the ebb and flow of private economic activity feed back on public spending and tax revenue.

The limited control by governments of budgetary outcomes results from the behavior of the different categories of spending and taxation. The spending of national governments falls into two accounting categories: 1) the part that funds goods and services for immediate use and 2) those expenditures over an extended period that create an asset which itself generates a flow of goods and services. The first category is usually named "current spending" and the latter "capital spending" or "investment spending." The US federal budget is unusual in that it makes no formal distinction between the two, though the categories are standard practice in the European Union and most countries across the globe.

These apparently straightforward categories, current and capital, prove problematical in concrete applica- tion. Most people would say that education creates an asset for the student, which increases income earn- ing potential into the future. Nonetheless, government accounts classify education as current expenditure. It could be argued that government budgets should include health care in the capital budget, since it is investment in human capacity to work. That argument is weaker than for education because public budgets have a "depre- ciation" category, and health services might fall into "maintenance" activity.

These disagreements over how to categorize dif- ferent expenditures derive from political and even philosophical predilections that need not divert us. How expenditures function in the budget provides a more practical guide, which gives three categories. The over- whelming majority of budgeted expenditures involve long-term commitments even if the outlays appear very short-term. These include all expenditures on services that the national political consensus judges as basic and necessary. Depending on the country, these might include education, health care, transport, communi- cations, public administration and national defense. Each item may be budgeted annually but in practice involves long-term commitments to society's welfare and cohesion.

In several countries in recent years, ideological predi- lections have provoked attempts at extreme reductions in the funding of public services. This has been the case especially in the United States at all levels of government, though also in the United Kingdom, with its much more centralized public funding system. Budget deficits, real or anticipated, serve as the frequent justification for these reductions. Such deficit-related arguments for spending cuts might be called "affordability" justifications, which come under scrutiny in the next myth ("We must tighten our belts").

Standardized statistics compiled by the Paris-based association of high-income countries, the Organisation for Economic Co-operation and Development, report that, in the mid-2010s, public expenditures on social services at all levels of government accounted for 19 percent of national income (or gross national product, GDP) in the United States; 22 to 25 percent in the United Kingdom, Japan and Germany; and considerably higher in France, at 32 percent (see http://stats.oecd.org). These expenditures make up our first category, long-term recurrent expenditures.

One-off multi-year projects in infrastructure and construction of social facilities such as schools and hospitals make up a second category of relatively stable expenditure. Projects begin and end, then new ones replace the completed ones. As one would expect, these expenditures account for a considerably smaller portion of national income than social expenditure. Such projects accumulate in a country's stock of productive assets, generating services and income over many years. If wisely planned, these projects "pay for themselves." The flow of repayment may assume direct cash form, such as tolls charged on motorways. More often the repayment is indirect, via taxes on the incomes the projects facilitate. Education provides a clear example.

Construction of schools and universities helps raise the general education of the population, which facilitates higher incomes and more tax revenue. In the mid-2010s, Japanese investment by all levels of government topped the league table among large developed countries, at 4 percent of national income, followed by France (3.5 percent), the United States (3 percent), Britain (2.5 percent) and Germany (surprisingly low, at barely 2 percent). Though relatively small in relation to the total economy, those expenditures sustain and expand the social infrastructure at the base of every society.

Expenditures linked to the health of the national economy give us a third, less obvious budget category. Discussions and debate over government budgets typically lump this with social expenditure, which is an analytical and practical mistake. Unemployment support shows how these expenditures operate. Imagine a small town with one large employer. Due to falling sales the company lays off half its employees. No longer receiving their wages and salaries, these employees and their families have less to spend. As a result, the local shops sell less, also reducing employment of their staff and perhaps closing in some cases. The initial lay-offs generate a downward spiral of less spending and less employment, which multiplies into a steep decline (which is why it is named the "multipliers process").

In part to prevent this cumulative effect that magnifies the initial loss of incomes from layoffs, in the early and middle decades of the twentieth century most governments introduced unemployment compensation programs. These programs initiate payments immediately when people become involuntarily unemployed – i.e., when they are unemployed due to circumstances beyond their control. In some countries, the United States is an example, these programs link to a specific tax ("Unemployment Insurance Contributions") and go into an earmarked fund. The more common practice is to fund them from general public revenue. The automatic nature of unemployment payments is their key characteristic, earning them the designation as an "automatic stabilizer."

Return to the small town example. The major employer lays off half its labor force. Close on the heels of their loss of income, the ex-employees receive unemployment compensation that partially replaces lost wages and salaries. As a result, spending by unemployed workers and their households falls less than would have been the case in the absence of the support payments. The initial layoffs generate a downward spiral of less spending, which is moderated when unemployment payments start automatically, reducing the fall in household spending (weakening the "multiplier process"). The local economy, and by extension the national economy, has been "automatically stabilized."

The effectiveness of the stabilizing effect, determined by how much compensation the unemployed receive and for how long, varies among countries. Accurate comparison across countries proves difficult because of differences in national legislation (and differences by state in the United States). According to a comparative study published by the International Labour Organization, in the early 2010s the "recipient ratios" (compensation as a percentage of last employment income) and the duration of payment for major countries were as follows: Germany, 88 percent and no time limit; United Kingdom, 64 percent for twelve months;

France, 56 percent for twenty-four months (for those younger than fifty; thirty-six months for those over fifty); United States, 27 percent for six months; and Japan, 23 percent for twelve months.

Politicians (and some economists) argue that unemployment compensation payments encourage unemployment. Whether this "misery fosters the work ethic" view is correct, it does not challenge the automatic stabilizing function of unemployment compensation. While it is paid to relatively few individuals, unemployment compensation provides an automatic cushion to protect the entire population from severe recessions – a few receive the payments and everyone gains from them. A political decision to weaken these programs by reducing compensation ratios and shortening payment periods may satisfy the ideological predilections of politicians and parts of the electorate. But doing so comes at considerable economic cost, magnifying mild downturns into recessions and recessions into depressions, harming the many by cuts in funding to the few.

The third category of expenditure, on automatic stabilizers, has an extremely important impact on the behavior of the public budget. Because these expenditures rise when the economy slows, they increase when tax revenue falls. A slowing economy means that household and business incomes increase at a slower rate or decline, because less is sold and fewer people have work. Loss of income results in lower tax payments. Simultaneously, unemployment payments increase.

The obvious result of less tax and more expenditure on unemployment support payments is a falling budget surplus or a deepening deficit. This combination – falling incomes and rising public deficits – manifested itself in every major country during the global recession of 2008–10. During these years, public deficits acted as a cushion for the economy. Falling tax and increasing support payments moderated economic collapse.

Unemployment support stands out as the most obvious automatic stabilizer, partially replenishing the incomes of the unemployed. Other public-sector stabilizers are rent subsidies (which rise as income falls); allowing early retirement (where a state pension partly replaces lost employment income); and various income-tested support programs (for example, the "Food Stamp" program in the United States and the much criticized "Universal Credit" in Britain). What all these have in common is that, to varying degrees, they act to reduce the fall in household incomes when the private economy dips into recession.

To the extent that it is characterized by progressive rates, the tax system itself serves an important automatic stabilizing role. This is obvious for the unemployed, whose work income falls to zero. Recipients of unemployment compensation pay tax on that replacement income, though proportionally less if income tax rates have a progressive structure. The more progressive the rate structure (the more rates rise as personal income rises), the more stabilizing will be the national revenue system. To state this effect more precisely, the more progressive a tax system, the less will be the fall in after-tax income compared to pre-tax income (tax falls more than take-home pay).

An example demonstrates this effect. Assume that a full-time employee receives an annual income of $50,000. Let the first $10,000 be tax-free ("exemptions"), the next $30,000 subject to a 15 percent tax and the next $10,000 to a rate of 25 percent. Total tax is $7,000 ($30,000 times 15 percent plus $10,000 times 25 percent = 4,500 + 2,500) – 14 percent of gross pay. Because of lack of sales demand, the company puts the employee on reduced hours, with the result that gross pay falls to $35,000. Pay falls by 30 percent (15/50). Applying the tax rate, we find that tax declines from $7,000 to $3,750 ($25,000 times 15 percent), or by over 45 percent.

When household income declines, perhaps as a result of a family member losing employment, tax obligation also declines. Were income tax rates strictly proportional – for example, 25 percent of income – income and tax would fall by the same amount. With a progressive income tax, as in the example, the household will drop into a lower tax "bracket," such as 15 percent. Tax obligation falls more than income: total household income might fall by $1,000 in the tax year and "disposable" income by less, perhaps $700 (depending on the tax rates and income width of the tax brackets).

Over the last several decades, national tax systems in Canada, the United States and Europe have become less progressive. This decline in progressivity resulted from changes in rates and, especially in the European Union, a shift from income taxes to sales-based taxes, the value added tax (VAT) being the most important. Sales-based taxes are regressive, rising slower than household incomes. The regressive nature of sales taxes results from their being flat-rate and because, in most countries, saving rates are near zero for all but high-income households. Research by Emmanuel Saez found that, in the early 2010s in the United States, the richest 1 percent saved about 40 percent of income, while the saving rate for the lowest 90 percent of households was close to zero. A flat-rate tax on spending in practice redistributes income to the richest.

Reducing the progressivity of a national tax system is a political choice. As for reducing unemployment compensation, it is a political choice that carries an economic cost. Both reduce the automatic stabilizing mechanisms by which the economy is protected against recession and inflation. The volatility of economies increases, making them more prone to recessionary contraction and inflationary over-heating. Inspecting types of spending and types of taxes leads to a clear conclusion. Except under unusual conditions, contraction and expansion of government deficits indicate the operation of the economy's automatic adjustments to sustain its health.

For two millennia, until well into the nineteenth century, medical science practiced blood-letting as treatment for certain types of human maladies. The practice derived from the Roman physician Galen, who thought that illness resulted from corruption of the blood. Medically induced bleeding contributed to the death of George Washington in 1799. Our analysis suggests that cutting spending to reduce a government budget deficit when the economy falls into recession – austerity policy – functions as the public policy equivalent of blood-letting. Analogously, austerity treats deficits as a problem (disease) solved by cutting (bleeding) the budget.

## *Why Do Governments Tax?*

The apparently sensible idea that governments tax to pay for spending is the basis of the conviction that governments should not run deficits, that they should "balance their books." Dispelling the first myth showed that "living within our means" is not binding on governments of countries with a national currency. These governments create their "means." Inspection of the second myth has to this point demonstrated that "balancing the books" is a very bad idea for a national government because it undermines the economy's capacity to correct itself, to adjust automatically in moments of instability.

If governments in countries with national currencies need not match revenue to spending, and if allowing the economy to adjust implies that they should not aim to match revenue to spending, what is the function of taxing people and businesses? No sensible person would advocate eliminating taxes and leaving the government to fund its spending by borrowing from the central bank or printing banknotes. But why? If a government doesn't have to "live within its means," and "balancing its books" is a bad idea, what are the guidelines governments should follow for spending and taxing? To develop the guidelines for spending and taxing I use a process of abstraction in which we begin with the simplest case ("abstracting" from complexities of reality) and move to the more realistic.

Imagine an economy with households and businesses but no government and no exports or imports. Numbers help clarify the example. Total goods and services in this simple economy equal $100 (or £/€/¥), all produced in businesses. The businesses distribute all their profits to households, so that the value of production equals household income (wages, salaries and dividends). The households spend ("consume") and save ("non-spending"). If households spend (consume) $70 and save $30, all goods and services will not be sold. Businesses will discover that $30 of goods and services remain in warehouses (for goods) or manifest themselves in idle employees (for services).

For everything produced to be sold, the $30 of saving by households must be balanced by someone else spending $30. That balancing comes from business investment. When businesses invest an amount equal to household saving, spending and production are equal – the economy has balanced its books. The economy reached that balance by one set of actors (households) lending to another (businesses). This simple balancing is shown in figure 2.1. The first scale is unbalanced. Spending (investment) exceeds non-spending (saving). That imbalance is manifested in shortages of all or some goods and services. If this simple economy has idle labor and idle productive capacity, the excessive demand will generate expansion of total production (growth of the economy). Production rises, household incomes rise, and increased household saving (non-spending) eliminates the excess demand to balance the national economy's books.

If there is no idle labor and productive capacity, production cannot expand, at least not in the immediate future. The excess demand (investment more than saving) creates shortages of goods and services. The shortages generate inflationary pressure, and the rising prices eliminate the excess demand. Because the value of

Economy with one part, private sector

Too much spending on domestic goods & services causing inflationary pressure

Spending on domestic goods & services balanced with non-spending economy stable

Not enough spending on domestic goods & services causing recessionary pressures

(non-spending) household saving

(spending) business investment

(non-spending) household saving

(spending) business investment

(non-spending) household saving

(spending) business investment

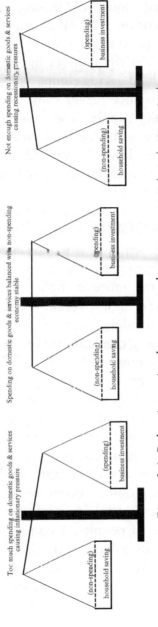

*Figure 2.1 Balancing a simple economy that has one part (a private sector)*

65

production equals household income, rising sales prices mean rising incomes. The inflationary rise in incomes generates the inflated savings that balance the economy.

The scale on the right shows the opposite result, an excess of household saving compared to business investment. This imbalance leaves some goods and services unsold, in excess supply. The excess supply is eliminated by businesses cutting back on production. Lower production means lower household incomes and lower saving. Falling household incomes bring the economy back into balance. In the middle sits a scale showing the economy balanced (household saving equals business investment), the result of expansion to eliminate excess demand or contraction to eliminate excess supply.

This simple example has established several insights that apply to the more complicated economies that follow. First, the economy reaches stability, neither contracting nor expanding, when everything produced is sold. The economy can stabilize by going up (expanding) or by going down (contracting). The balancing of the economy is an automatic adjustment (something that happens on its own). The level at which it stabilizes can leave us with unacceptable unemployment, with undesirable inflation or in some intermediate position. Second, saving by one person, group or economic institution must be exactly compensated by spending by another person, group or economic institution. Third, and this is also completely general, the value of production is made up of people's incomes. A fall or rise in prices corresponds to an equal fall or rise in incomes. This is an important relationship that will reappear when we consider the effects of inflation.

At this point the second insight needs further emphasis. It can be restated as follows: if an economic actor A spends less than its income ("saves"), there must be an economic actor B that spends more than its income ("dis-saves"), and the As and Bs must cancel each other. If they do not cancel each other, the economy either declines (goods and services go unsold) or expands (a shortage of goods and services induces more production).

In a step towards greater realism, let this economy open to trade with other countries. It helps understanding this more complicated case if we hold tight to the insight that the economy stabilizes, "balances its books," when spending and non-spending are equal. In this slightly more realistic economy, households have three options for their incomes. They can buy domestic goods and services, buy goods and services from other countries, and save – spend domestically, import, and not spend. The $100 in household income now divides into $50 spent on domestic goods and services, $20 on imports (total spending still $70), and $30 saved. Spending on imports, like saving, does not add to the demand for domestic production (it is demand for production in other countries). In this new scheme, businesses for their part can sell their goods and services to households or to foreigners (export).

We can apply our earlier insights to our more complicated economy (figure 2.2). For the economy to reach stability, everything produced domestically must be sold. Households now spend $50 on domestic production, implying that the other $50 must be bought by domestic businesses or foreign households and businesses. Economic balance results when the saving ($30) and imports ($20) by households match domestic investment ($30) and exports ($20). In this numerical

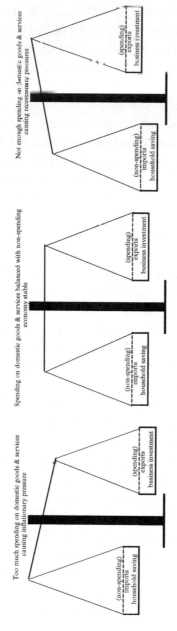

*Figure 2.2 Balancing a more complete economy that has two parts (a private sector and an external sector)*

case, household saving and business investment are equal and trade is balanced ($20 for imports and $20 for exports). In the real world this outcome would be very unusual. In general, countries have trade surpluses (exports exceed imports – for example, Germany) or trade deficits (imports exceed exports – for example, the United Kingdom and the United States).

That bit of reality introduces another slight but important complication, the implications of imbalance in the domestic sector and the external sector. Let there be a trade deficit, in which household imports rise to $25, household domestic spending falls to $45, and exports are unchanged at $20. This change in the numbers threatens to contract the economy. Domestic consumption plus business investment plus exports ($45 + $30 + 20 = $95) is less than domestic goods and services ($100). Now, $5 in goods and services go unsold.

A recession is in store for our imaginary economy. Recession is avoided and the economy's books are balanced by businesses increasing their investment spending to $35. The economy stabilizes with a trade deficit (imports at $25, exports at $20) because businesses increase their borrowing. Businesses brought the economy into balance by borrowing more to spend more. How the trade deficit is covered, "paid for," becomes clear in the busting of the next myth.

The case of a trade deficit allows us to state the second insight in more general form. For the economy to achieve stability, non-spending by households on domestic production, be it through saving or importing, must be exactly matched by other groups' spending (businesses and demand by foreigners). The economy now has two parts or sectors, an internal (domestic) part and an external (foreign) part. The two parts need not independently be in balance. Household saving need not match business investment, and imports need not match exports. Balance is regained when the total spent equals what is not spent across the two sectors.

If the economy has a trade deficit (as in the US and the UK), then the domestic private sector must run a spending surplus (business investment will exceed household saving). The reverse applies to a trade surplus: household saving will exceed business investment. To put the condition in the language of budget morality, if one part of the economy is frugal, another part must be profligate.

Now, we can bring government into our imaginary economy so that it has three parts – private sector, external sector and public sector. The big analytical jump was from the one-sector example to the two-sector case. Moving from two to three merely involves changing the arithmetic. The economy now balances its books (seeks stability) when the domestic spending and non-spending across the three parts add up to zero. In detail, this means that household saving, plus tax, plus imports adjust to match the sum of business investment, government spending, and export demand. This book balancing appears in the three-sector scale in figure 2.3.

We are now very close to discovering our taxation guideline. We take the three sectors one by one. Even if it were possible, no one would suggest that businesses should be constrained by the requirement that their investments be no more or no less than household saving. This constraint applies only in the ultra-simple, stripped-down, one-sector example. The development of investment banks in the nineteenth century liberated

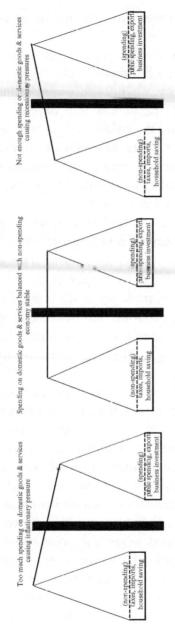

Economy with three parts, private sector, external sector & public sector

Too much spending on domestic goods & services causing inflationary pressure

(non-spending) taxes, imports, household saving

(spending) public spending, export business investment

Spending on domestic goods & services balanced with non-spending economy stable

(non-spending) taxes, imports, household saving

(spending) public spending, export business investment

Not enough spending or domestic goods & services causing recessionary pressures

(non-spending) taxes, imports, household saving

(spending) public spending, export business investment

*Figure 2.3  Balancing a complete three-part economy (a private sector, an external sector and a public sector)*

businesses from their investments being constrained by private saving.

Similarly, no one but an extreme xenophobe would advocate a "balanced trade" rule. The ebb and flow of economic activity, changes in international conditions, and many other influences will determine a country's trade balance and the balance of private-sector spending and saving (the "internal balance"). Public expenditure and tax revenue serve as the instruments to achieve the balance sought by government policy.

The outcomes for the private sector are beyond the power of households and businesses to predict, much less determine. Saving and imports move up and down as the economy adjusts to a stable level of production and income. Deficits or surpluses in the domestic private sector and in trade are neither good nor bad. They result when the economy adjusts to changes in circumstances. The compensating movements in the different sectors show clearly in the concrete numbers from the real economies.

In buoyant times, businesses can sell the goods and services they produce. If the expansion persists, an increasing number of businesses will discover that their production comes closer to capacity limits. This provokes new investment in machinery and buildings, as well as hiring and training more staff. The reverse occurs when expansion ends and pressure on capacity ends. It follows that, as a general pattern, businesses borrow and invest when the economy expands, then curtail their enthusiasm for greater capacity when expansion turns into stagnation or recession. Since the borrowing comes from financial institutions, we should expect a pattern in which bank lending increases during expansion and slows or contracts when the economy and markets for goods and services cease to grow.

The categories "borrowing" and "lending" also apply to central government budgets. As explained earlier, when a government falls into deficit, it becomes a borrower, either from the private sector by bond auctions or from its central bank (intra-government borrowing). A surplus functions as lending (or "negative borrowing") when the government buys back its bonds and passes cash to the private sector or its central bank. Most governments do not produce goods and services for commercial sale. Rather, their mandate requires them to generate public services in good times and bad. As a result, when the economy slows and contracts, a central government tends to become a borrower at the moment when the private sector curtails its investments and banks reduce their lending.

Figure 2.4 demonstrates that these relationships are not merely logical possibilities; they manifest themselves quite concretely. It uses a simple presentation technique that facilitates discovering whether two sets of numbers increase together or move in opposite directions (whether they are positively or negatively paired). The vertical axis takes the case of UK public-sector borrowing (the budget deficit is a positive number). The horizontal axis shows the lending by UK financial corporations (mostly commercial banks). For financial corporations, lending is also a positive number. If public borrowing (the deficit) increased when financial lending increased, the two sets of numbers would approximate a straight line starting near zero and increasing towards the right as one looks at the graph – more public borrowing, more

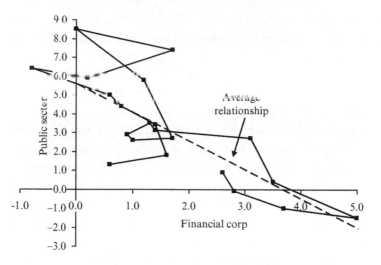

*Figure 2.4 Automatic stabilization of the UK economy,
public and private lending/borrowing, 1991–2017
(percentages of GDP)*
Source: UK Office for National Statistics.

financial lending (more borrowing by non-financial companies to invest).

We discover the opposite, as explained ("predicted") in the discussion above. When the economy is buoyant, the number of loans and the amount of business borrowing increase (to the right along the horizontal line) as the public budget deficit declines. In the opposite circumstance, recession, the public deficit rises as business borrowing (financial lending) contracts. Figure 2.4 is a numerical verification of the diagrams using the scale metaphor, which corresponds to the real functioning of the private and public sector. It is a visual demonstration of the automatic stabilizing process explained earlier in this chapter.

The same compensating movements in private and public borrowing and lending apply to other economies. Showing the equivalent of figure 2.4 for the US economy proves much more complicated because of bond financing of nominally non financial businesses, especially large corporations. Over the first two decades of this century, many if not most large corporations have become "financialized," issuing their own debt paper, "junk bonds," to finance investments. Less long-term bank lending to businesses represents the flipside of this financialization process.

The compensating interaction of public deficits and private borrowing takes us back to the insight that economies can stabilize at low or high levels of production and income. An economy can find itself stuck at unacceptably high rates of unemployment combined with underutilization of productive equipment. These symptoms of recession result from depressed business investment and inadequate export demand. In these circumstances the economy is limited by demand. The opposite problem, excessively robust private-sector spending and buoyant export demand, can provoke inflationary pressures. These pressures can have two unsustainable results, the most obvious being destabilizing price increases. If the government does not impose import restrictions, the more likely outcome is an unsustainable trade imbalance.

The function of tax now jumps out as so obvious that in retrospect the long discussion in this section may seem unnecessary. Households spend and save to advance the welfare of their members. Businesses invest and borrow to advance the collective welfare of their stockholders. Democratically legitimate governments spend and tax to advance the collective welfare of their citizens. To provide the social services needed by citizens, governments spend. Governments tax to prevent the economy from sinking into recession or expanding excessively into inflation.

The tax guideline really is that simple. An example demonstrates the simple validity of the guideline. It begins with the three-sector economy in low unemployment and low inflation, with public expenditure at a level to cover citizen demand for social services. Due to global instability, business expectations of future sales and profits collapse, causing a substantial fall in private investment. To compensate for the contraction in private spending, the government must increase the demand generated by the public budget. It does this by selecting the tax structure – types of tax and rates – which will yield the revenue level that will re-establish an adjustment to low unemployment with manageable inflation.

Generating less revenue fulfils the purpose of that new tax structure, to "balance the books" of the economy, as in the middle (balanced) scale of the three-part economy shown in figure 2.3. The collapse of business investment caused a spending deficit in the private economy. With export demand also weak, it falls to the government to reset the balance by selecting and implementing the appropriate tax regime. Once the reset is done, the production and incomes recover. Recovering production and incomes bit by bit brings the private sector back to health.

Whether the new economy-balancing tax regime results in a public budget deficit or a surplus is of the same importance as whether private investment is in deficit or surplus with private saving and whether trade is in deficit or surplus. These three sectors interact. One should not be considered in isolation from the others. What appears as an undesirable outcome with the public budget (a deficit) results from a problem in the private sector (weak investment); the former compensates for the latter.

Let us begin a second example as we did the first. The three-sector economy has low unemployment and low inflation, with public expenditure set to cover citizen demand for social services. Due to a global commodity boom, business expectations of future sales and profits rise, causing a substantial increase in investment. The increased business investment threatens to generate inflation. To compensate for the expansion in private spending, the government must decrease the demand contribution of the public budget. This is achieved by a reset of the tax structure that increases revenue. Once the reset is done, the production and incomes grow more slowly. Slower growth of production and incomes adjust the private sector back towards non-inflationary balance bit by bit.

Why do governments tax? They tax to balance the books of our economy at low unemployment and low inflation. In the real world of managing public budgets, the choice between adjusting expenditure and adjusting tax evolves in a pragmatic manner. For clarity of exposition I have presumed public expenditures fixed by political decision, implying an appropriate tax level. In practice the two interact.

## *From Myth to Reality*

For a government implementing sound economic policy, the function of taxation is to manage the national economy – balance the economy's books. Sound policy sets the level of tax revenue to avoid the dangers of recession, on the one hand, and excessive inflation, on the other. Governments spend to provide services to citizens. Governments tax to keep the economy in the safe region between excessive unemployment and excessive inflation.

Astronomers have coined the term "Goldilocks Zone" to refer to the distance from a star in which the conditions for life (as we know it) are met. In "Goldilocks and the Three Bears" the little girl encounters three bowls of porridge, three chairs and three beds. Having tested them, she rejects two and judges the last in each case as "just right." Specifically with regard to the porridge, she finds one bowl too hot and one too cold, with the third just right. Following astronomers, we can apply Goldilocks's judgments to economies, as in figure 2.5. Sound budget management has the goal of maintaining a combination of low unemployment and low inflation, the economy's Goldilocks Zone.

If public-sector spending and tax leave the economy short of demand, we find ourselves with excessive unemployment ("too cold," to quote Goldilocks). If the public budget generates excessive demand, inflation results ("too hot"). The public sector must play this economy-balancing role because neither households nor businesses can. The inability of private institutions to do so comes as an inherent consequence of the lack of a coordinating

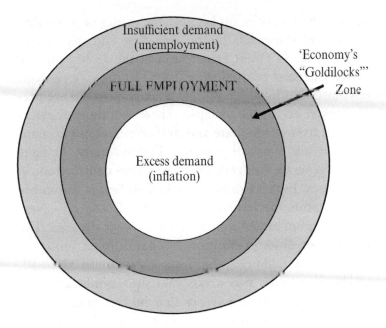

*Figure 2.5 Managing the economy into the Goldilocks Zone*

mechanism across households and the business sector. This lack of private coordination in market economies has its benefits, such as the flexibility to move labor and finance across the range of economic activities and the closely related processes of competition and innovation. These benefits come at a potentially high cost – instability of the economy. Economic management through adjusting the public budget provides the mechanism to reduce the systemic instability of market economies.

We should not place excessive faith in the ability of public budget management to keep our economy in the Goldilocks Zone. Circumstances arise when budget policy cannot realize the goals of low unemployment and low inflation. The failure of budget policy to achieve them may result because the causes of instability lie beyond the reach of the spending and tax instruments. The US Great Depression in the 1930s and the global financial crisis during 2008–10 provide obvious circumstances in which budget management did not prevent severe economic collapse. These economic disasters resulted from inadequate and dysfunctional public management of financial sectors. Expansionary budgets helped generate recovery after disastrous contractions in both cases. In the 1930s in the United States, a number of prevention mechanisms in Franklin Roosevelt's New Deal program tamed financial markets for decades. The removal of those prevention mechanisms set loose the forces that would bring the Great Recession of 2008–10.

The possibility also arises that no Goldilocks Zone exists or else it is so narrow that budget management proves too blunt an instrument to keep the economy inside it. To understand when and why that possibility arises, we need to clarify the nature and causes of inflation, which is done in the dispelling of the last myth ("there is no alternative").

The deficits and debt associated with the Goldilocks guide to spending and taxes are sustainable except in unusual circumstances that are fully discussed in the dispelling of other myths. Understanding the Goldilocks principle of economic management, generally accepted as sound policy for three decades after World War II, requires no technical jargon and no algebra, though the latter can be useful.

When we overcome the tax-to-spend myth, economic policy becomes much simpler to understand than decoding the polemics of austerity. Casting off the tax-to-spend myth allows the citizen to recognize positive

benefits of deficits and debt when governments practice sound economic management (developed under
Myth 3). Post-myth clarity on tax creates "eureka
moments" that explain other issues every citizen should
understand: inflation, employment, public services and
fostering equity.

The difficulties of managing the economy take us
back to the earlier discussion of designing policy so it
can be reversed. It is useful to repeat that discussion in
the context of the Goldilocks Zone. Assume the economy is "too cold" and policy makers decide to increase
expenditure and fund that expenditure by selling bonds
to the private sector. The hoped-for expansion proves
stronger than anticipated, pushing the economy into
the inflation zone. Selling the bonds that funded the
expansion to the private sector provides an instrument
to reverse or dampen it, because bond sales transfer cash
from the private to the public sector, which depresses
private spending.

If the government had funded its increased spending
by directly granting itself credit from the central bank,
it would have no reversal instrument. The only available "way out" of the excessive expansion would be tax
increases or expenditure cuts. Both of these tend to be
slow working and administratively more complicated
than the simplicity of bond sales and purchases.

# 3

# We Must Tighten Our Belts

*The Myth Itself*

A national government with its own currency should manage taxes in order to keep the economy near full utilization of resources while avoiding a destabilizing inflation rate. When business investment surges buoyantly and exports boom, the appropriate taxation to achieve the balance between near maximum resource and desired inflation is likely to generate a budget surplus. When business activity flounders and the world economy generates weak export demand, a budget deficit is the likely outcome, striking the "Goldilocks balance" of high employment and low inflation.

For several advanced economies, the late 1990s and early 2000s represented the former case, with both the British and American governments posting strong budget surpluses. The global crisis beginning in 2008 brought the end of private-sector booms, ushering in a period of public-sector deficits across the globe; these reached levels not seen for decades, in some cases not since World War II.

Excluding the already mentioned United Kingdom, in 2007 eleven EU countries ran budget surpluses, and the average for all twenty-six was close to balance at minus 0.2 percent of GDP, hardly different from zero (a balanced budget). In 2009 the average fell to minus 6.5 percent, and not one government budget showed a surplus. In the United States, in Britain and across the EU, politicians of most parties raised anxieties about "living within our means." These anxieties led to a perceived urgency to reduce deficits, for countries and their populations to "tighten their belts," a cliché conveying the message that governments could not afford such imbalances between revenue and expenditure.

Looking back to the war years provides an insight into this affordability argument and the management of public budgets. At the depth of the global financial crisis in 2009–10 the US public-sector deficit briefly reached 10 percent of national income (look back at figure 0.1, p. 8). The same years brought a similar deficit level in the United Kingdom. Those 10 percent deficits look minor compared to the budget imbalances in both countries during the years 1941 to 1945. In the United States the federal government deficit ballooned to almost 30 percent of GDP in 1943–4, and the figure was only slightly less for the British government. During those years no American or British politician argued that the war was "unaffordable"; none suggested that the deficits were so excessive that their governments should capitulate because of reckless expenditure.

Of course, those were literally life or death struggles that justified whatever budgeting measures were necessary to sustain the war effort: democratically elected governments applied budget measures necessary for rare and extreme circumstances. Most people did indeed "tighten their belts" during the war years. National priorities prompted that belt-tightening, not a perceived urgency to balance budgets. The principle that public budgets should reflect society's priorities applies in peace and in normal times as it did in the rare and extreme times of war. That principle demonstrates the fallacy of the belt-tightening argument.

## The Affordability Fallacy

The belt-tightening argument is an assertion about what a government can afford to spend. The affordability argument is a fallacy, a close cousin to our first myth, "living within our means." The message seems reasonable enough on the surface: our government has a limited budget, we must live within it, and we cannot afford to over-run it. It is likely that "afford" in this context first strikes the reader or listener as having a purely monetary or financial meaning. Taxes are the source of our government's funding, producing a finite amount of public revenue during any budget period. Spending more than the budgeted amount is living beyond our means. Since the government must balance its books, any project that over-runs the budget is not affordable, no matter how commendable.

The first two myth-busting chapters disposed of this, the narrow financial interpretation of affordability. National governments that manage their own currencies do not confront fixed budgets. They create their "means" either through increased tax or borrowing. The increased tax need not come from higher tax rates. Expansion of our economy automatically generates more revenue. If the government assesses the need for greater expenditure as too urgent to await economic expansion, it can borrow. If immediate borrowing by the sale of public bonds in capital markets appears too expensive because the interest rates would be too high, the central bank exists as a backup purchaser.

Reflection suggests the intention of a deeper meaning of the words "afford" and "affordability." Often we find them used to convey a message about fundamental social and economic changes that impact not only on governments but on society as a whole. The deeper meaning fosters an apprehension that we may find ourselves in the grip of forces beyond our control that have profound implications for the role of our governments.

A prominent example of the deeper message of affordability begins with the indisputable assertion that, in many countries, especially the countries with relatively high average incomes, the population is ageing. Also indisputable is that at some point the income earning of elderly people ends, to be replaced by public and private pensions. In the twenty-first century elderly people live long enough to draw pension payments for an extended period, which in itself is a good thing: people are living longer. However, even though pensions are taxed, the shift of adults from taxpayer to pension recipient impacts on tax revenue. This reduced tax effect goes along with elderly people generating a high demand for public services, especially care services.

This combination allegedly places an unaffordable burden on pension funds and health services. Adding to

85

this affordability argument is the fact that ageing-related public expenditures burden the working population, which must generate more tax revenue to fund the pensions and the health care of the old. Care for those no longer able to look after themselves presents a potentially large expense for the public sector. In consequence, the ageing of the population must inevitably mean that our government cannot afford full care of the elderly plus their pensions. The elderly or their families must pay part, perhaps a growing part, as the ageing of the population continues.

Logicians name this type of argument a "syllogism." One of the most famous examples is

> Dogs are animals,
> humans are animals,
> therefore dogs are human.

Myths of public spending and taxation derive their verisimilitude from similar syllogisms reinforced by ambiguous metaphors. These construct an edifice of misunderstanding that must be deconstructed in order to allow for understanding.

The ageing argument for reducing social services is quite easily exposed as a syllogism, providing a useful path to refute the affordability fallacy in general. Since the beginning of humankind people have passed through the cycle of birth, childhood, adulthood, old age and death. Throughout human existence societies have managed this cycle by able-bodied adults caring for children and the elderly. This occurs in all but pathologically degenerate societies. Someone who stigmatizes this fundamental characteristic of all societies as a "burden on

86

the young" suffers from a serious antisocial personality disorder; he or she is a "sociopath."

The purveyors of this argument might protest that they recognize the life cycle phenomenon that requires the young to support the old, but that "society is ageing." This creates the long-term problem that fewer and fewer able-bodied adults must support more and more non-working children and elderly people. This, too, is a transparent syllogism, for two obvious reasons. One reason emerged during the 2016 US presidential primary campaign when a journalist suggested to Vermont Senator Bernie Sanders that he was excessively old to seek the nomination, because he was "going to be seventy-two." The senator promptly answered, "Everyone is going to be seventy-two."

Whatever the relevance of the senator's answer to an election campaign, therein lies a deep truth, that everyone ages (except an unfortunate few who die young), and that those currently young will become old. If our population held in a steady distribution of children, able-bodied adults and the elderly, the "burden on the youth" argument would be almost impossible to maintain, because people would pass through the phases of life at a steady rate.

The population is ageing, goes the second part of the affordability argument, so the burden of the old on the young increases over time. Those who are young must support more children and elderly than was the case for those who are now elderly, and "that's not fair." Some have dubbed this phenomenon the "demographic time bomb." The online businessdictionary.com describes this in the following way: "As the dependency ratio rises, the income of the working segment . . . of a population comes under increasing pressure to provide support for the non-working . . . segment."

This second part of the argument, that those young now must pay more tax than did the older generation, is as obviously invalid as the first part. Empirical evidence indicates that the "bomb" turns out to have no explosives in it. The important statistic for this argument is neither the average age of our population nor the share of the population over a specific age such as sixty-five or seventy. What determines whether working youngsters must bear an increasing weight of non-working oldsters is the "labor force participation rate" (LFPR). The standard calculation of the LFPR is those employed plus those unemployed and looking for work divided by the potential working population, usually measured as those who are fifteen years or older (the World Bank, an international development organization, provides such information at https://data.worldbank.org).

Obvious "demographic bomb" candidate countries are France, Germany, Great Britain, the United States and Japan, all of which have populations whose average age is increasing. Notwithstanding that increasing trend, for three of those five the LFPR has hardly changed over twenty-five years. In France from 1990 to 2015 the participation statistic declined slightly, from 55.7 to 55.2 percent. For the United Kingdom the shift was also insubstantial, from 62.6 to 62.2 percent. In the United States it did fall, though not greatly, from 63.4 to 62.2 percent. In ageing Germany over those same years the LFPR actually increased, from 58.3 to 60.4 percent. That increase occurred despite the largest rise in the share of the population over sixty-five, from 14.9 to 21.4 percent. Among the five, only in Japan do we find a substantial fall in labor force participation, from 65.4 to 60.4 percent.

Yet again we have a striking example of a common-sense inference – ageing populations mean a burden on the young – revealed as flat-earth reasoning. The inference is wrong in practice for many reasons, not least because of governments increasing the minimum age to receive state pensions and eliminating ageist enforced retirement laws. The myth is that ageing populations increase the burden of the non-productive elderly. The truth is that, when people live longer, they work longer.

A few statistics reinforce that conclusion. Figure 3.1 shows public-sector spending on retirement pensions for six high income countries, four in the European Union, plus Japan and the United States. To make the statistics easily comparable, each country's pension share in GDP is set to an index of 100 in 1991. The values at the end of the time period are reported in the legend. For example, in 2013 Italy had the largest pension share of GDP, at 16.3 percent, and the United Kingdom had the lowest, at 6.1 percent. The countries are listed in order of the increase in the index over the twenty-three years. The starting year is chosen because it marked the unification of Germany (before which statistics are not comparable), and the last year was the most recent from the OECD database.

Three conclusions jump from figure 3.1. First, in only one of these ageing countries – Japan – did the pension share increase dramatically. As should be obvious, that was not because the Japanese population aged at a dramatically faster rate than the population in other countries. It was the result in part of a relatively low retirement age in Japan compared to the other countries.

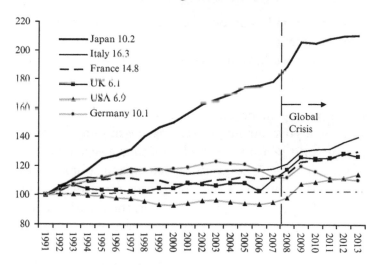

*Figure 3.1 Public pension payments in six high-income countries, 1991–2013*

*Note:* Index of share of GDP all set so 1991 =100, with 2013 share in legend.
*Source:* Organisation for Economic Co-operation and Development (https://dataoecd.org).

The second striking conclusion from the figure is that, in the other five countries, the pension share hardly changed during the ten years before the global crisis. And, third, in every country except the United States, the global crisis coincided with a marked increase in the pension share. This last observation indicates one of the important coping mechanisms for older workers who lost their jobs when the crisis hit: taking early retirement as allowed under these national pension systems.

Upon inspection, the numbers indicate that none of the countries has experienced an out-of-control demographic boom. They convey two simpler, more straightforward tales: first, providing pensions for the elderly is a political choice by society; and, second, an ageing population is a benefit to, not a burden on, society, allowing the entire population to live longer, work longer and retire with dignity.

What if the "demographic bomb" had had some explosive in it, and, indeed, the non-income-earning elderly grew faster than the income-generating group? Even where that occurs it would not provide a valid argument for the non-affordability of state pensions. The affordability myth functions as a red herring. It disguises a political argument as a technical necessity.

Let us go back to the basics discussed above. In all societies the young care for the old. As societies become larger and more complex in their division of labor, the elderly receive this care less within the family and more through institutions specifically constructed for that purpose. Looking after elderly people who require aid for everyday tasks can occur in families, but in high-income countries this care increasingly occurs in institutions, what in my childhood were dubbed "old age homes."

These institutions can be part of the public or the private sector. Because the institution will do much the same things whether public or private, the cost is likely to be much the same for a given quality of care. The commitment of a civilized society to provide adequate care for the elderly determines the total cost. The extent to which the public or private sector provides the means to fulfill that commitment is a political decision. In making this decision, labor force participation rates, dependency rates and intergenerational burdens are irrelevant.

We can imagine the policy process going as follows.

91

1   Do we as citizens commit ourselves to ensure that, with as few exceptions as possible, elderly citizens have a healthy and dignified retirement? The political answer may be, "no, that is the responsibility of each family." Most would consider a political choice resulting in the rationing of health and dignity by household income to be callous. If collectively we make the opposite political decision, to honor the social commitment to care for the elderly, a second question arises.

2   To what level of healthy and dignified retirement do we commit ourselves? As a practical matter our government will implement that collective commitment, though not necessarily only through private institutions. Be the institutions public or private, it falls to our government to ensure full and non-discriminatory access, to regulate health and safety, and to monitor performance. The wealth of society ultimately determines the level at which our government can implement the commitment. Societies in countries with high average incomes possess both the technical knowledge to provide a high level of care and a level of income and wealth to fund that care.

3   After we make a collective judgment about the desired level and coverage of care, we confront the political decision concerning funding, whether it should be public or private. To be specific, we face a decision about the amount of care to finance by taxation of ourselves and the amount to purchase from market providers.

The political choice between funding by tax and private funding has no impact on "saving money" or shifting "burdens." Consider an example. A family includes an elderly member no longer able to carry out the routine of daily life. This elderly person moves into a care home that is funded through taxation. After an election the new government announces that it has sold the care home to a private corporation. In the future the elderly residents must pay for all their care. The elderly residents or their relatives begin paying for what previously was funded by taxation.

In the example, the consequence of the privatization of elderly care is to change the form of the household's payments from taxation to direct payment to the private care provider. If household incomes were equally distributed, the total care cost was the same for public and private provision, and the quality of care was also the same, a shift from taxation to direct private payment would involve a mere shift in funding method.

In no country, wealthy or poor, are household incomes equally distributed. In all wealthy countries the tax system is progressive: the higher the household income, the larger is the share paid in tax. Taxation provides the vehicle to fund a standard service of care that fulfills the commitment to full and non-discriminatory coverage. It is a method to counter the inequality generated by market economies.

The shift from public to private funding does not alter the total cost of the commitment to universal coverage. Total funding declines only if 1) private provision comes at a price lower than the public equivalent; 2) coverage declines by exclusion of parts of the population; or 3) the standard of care declines. Using an example with numbers helps clarify the point. As a round figure, let each person in care require medication costing the public sector 1,000 per month (dollars, pounds, euros). In a partial privatization measure the government passes legislation to limit monthly coverage of medication to 500.

This change would appear to "save the taxpayer" 500 per patient in care. It does not. The 500 that the public sector no longer pays generates far greater cost than the expenditure reduction. Some families will lack the income to make up the 500 cut from the provision of medications. As a result, some patients will develop maladies previously prevented, causing other care costs and for many an earlier death. The apparent saving in practice saves nothing. Its cost is lost from view because it is not revealed in immediate monetary form.

### Social Protection and Equity

The affordability argument against public spending has flaws in logic and practice. Affordability should always refer to society as a whole. How society divides provision between public and private is a political choice. Many if not most people might accept the fallacy of affordability arguments against public spending yet reject universal provision on other grounds. We frequently encounter the opinion that universal public provision can result in benefits going to those who "do not need them." Even if public provision comes in at lower cost, why should the taxpayer fund services for those who can afford to pay? This version of the affordability argument appears to stress equity. If a person or household has an income above that of the average taxpayer, universal provision would appear to involve

94

a regressive redistribution from the average taxpayer to the wealthy taxpayers.

The alternative to universal provision of public services is some exclusion rule. The exclusion rule for most non universal public services involves some form of income testing. Governments rarely use this approach in the provision of services for primary and secondary schooling, though it is frequently applied to social protection programs involving cash payments. Advocates of this approach to delivering public services, usually called "means testing" or "income testing," justify it by using equity and effectiveness arguments.

Stated briefly, advocates of restricting access to social protection argue that an income criterion directs benefits to those who need them and does not waste funding on those who can afford to purchase the services. The word "targeting" frequently appears in this context – to be efficient and effective, social benefits should target the relevant recipients. This argument usually draws the inference that targeting – restricting access – allows more funding for those "who really need it."

For some social benefits targeting is not only appropriate but the purpose of the program. Disability benefits should go to those who are disabled; veterans' health services to veterans; child benefits to children; and so on. All of these refer to what we might call categorical programs. They do not involve an income criterion, though they could. Veterans' benefits could in practice have two criteria – having served in the military and incomes less than a specified level. However, in practice, applying an income exclusion criterion proves considerably more difficult in practice than categorical exclusion.

People across the political spectrum agree that access

to many public services cannot involve an income or any other exclusion rule. Governments could not set tests for access to activities such as fire-fighting, general policing and national defense. Either everyone enjoys the protection against fire or the service cannot fulfill its mandate, putting out fires. If my neighbor's house burns, it threatens mine; a theft next door could occur in my home next time; and no national defense system could operate selectively.

Setting aside these collective and indivisible activities such as fire-fighting, the answer to the rhetorical question "Why provide free services to those able to pay?" proves not obvious for several reasons. The delivery of numerous public activities could have access targeted by income, but do not. The governments of almost every country provide free primary education for all, notwithstanding that high-income households can and do purchase education from private institutions. Almost every advanced country delivers universal health care through various institutional vehicles, although the United States remains an exception.

Most European countries have free access to public transport for specific categories of the population, most frequently the elderly and students. These categorical benefits involve an important principle. They differ from those mentioned above (e.g., military veterans' benefits) in that the service involved does not directly link to the targeted group. Difficulties in physical mobility do not motivate governments to provide free access to public transport for the elderly. Mobility problems involve a separate, specialized service. Governments allow free access to public transport because of a political goal to reduce the social isolation of the elderly. Analogously, primary and secondary students enjoy free access to transport in several European countries with the purpose of reducing absentee rates – it makes traveling to school easier. In a few countries university students enjoy free transport.

No tuition charges for primary and secondary schooling and free access to transport provide examples of a general social value common across countries. Open, unrestricted access to some activities benefits everyone, not just those who take advantage of the benefit. Vaccinations provide a non-controversial example. We all benefit from the eradication of a disease, and realizing that benefit requires vaccinating everyone. Until recently a near consensus existed in most countries that a well-educated population benefits everyone, both for national economic success as a result of a more productive workforce and for social stability because a more discerning electorate will prove less prone to extremes (or so one hopes). Functionalist arguments frequently provide the basis for other cases of universal coverage. Workplace-linked health-care programs may limit the mobility of employees, while universal coverage facilitates moving between jobs.

Thus we find many public programs that do not use income testing, and not doing so generates no demands that those who can afford it should not benefit. Primary and secondary education provides the most obvious cases. The anxiety that universal provision will reinforce inequalities has a straightforward solution – progressive taxation. If high-income households benefit by sending children to publicly funded schools, an appropriately designed tax system can recapture that benefit several times over. We can state the general principle succinctly:

"equal provision for all funded by progressive taxation, justified by the social gain achieved."

At least three further considerations support universal provision as a rational method of public-service provision – cost-effectiveness, social cohesion and reducing inequality. Categorical forms of targeting carry very low administrative costs because identification is the central access issue. Benefits for veterans require proof of military service; bus passes for over-sixties a birth certificate or equivalent; and similarly for benefits accruing to expectant mothers, children and students. All these involve once-and-for-all identification. Identification costs for those with disabilities can prove somewhat more costly and repetitive, especially if benefit-cutting drives government policy, an accusation raised against Conservative governments in the United Kingdom after 2010.

By contrast, the administrative costs of income-tested programs can be quite substantial. The UK Universal Credit support system, introduced by the Conservative government in 2013, provides an extreme example. According to the UK National Audit Office, the administrative cost of a claim by a recipient (or appeal against a government decision) had an average cost of £700. The monthly payment in the same year was £252 for a single claimant and £500 for two joint claimants.

More important than administrative cost may be the political and societal impact of means testing. While universal provision unites society by making everyone a beneficiary, means testing explicitly divides society. The terminology of the division may seem formally neutral – recipients and non-recipients – but it quickly becomes judgmental, laden with political ideology. In the United

Kingdom some politicians use the terms "shirkers" and "strivers," while in the United States phrases such as "free riders" and "welfare fakers" express similar contempt. The unsuccessful US presidential candidate Mitt Romney famously epitomized the "them and-us" view of means testing in a now infamous speech to a group of wealthy political donors on 17 May 2012:

> There are 47 percent of the people who will vote for the president [Barack Obama] no matter what. All right, there are 47 percent who are ... dependent upon government, who believe that they are victims, who believe the government has a responsibility to care for them, who believe that they are entitled to health care, to food, to housing, to you name it.

This characterization of recipients of social benefits follows the perverse logic of means testing. In order to access the benefits, people must accept a government-defined status which in practice stigmatizes them as outsiders. The stigma becomes formal through a verification process frequently demeaning by its intrusiveness. Verification functions in effect as the policing of the poor, requiring a large bureaucracy to determine repeatedly who qualifies and who does not. The stigma becomes all the more obvious when low-income status overlaps with ethnic identify, which reinforces stereotyping.

Universal access to benefits avoids the social divisiveness inherent in income or means testing. Also, contrary to what one might think, universal access proves a powerful vehicle for reducing inequality. Figure 3.2 shows average incomes of households across quintiles in the United Kingdom and the United States. It reports the ratio of "original" income (before income tax) to

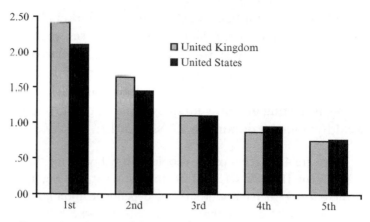

*Figure 3.2 Ratio of disposable income to original income, United Kingdom and United States, by quintiles, 2014*

Note: Original income includes earnings and private pensions; disposable income is original income, plus cash benefits, minus income tax.
Source: US Congressional Budget Office and UK Office for National Statistics.

"disposable" income (after income tax) for each fifth of the population. Original income (the UK term; "market income" is the US category) includes in both countries earned income plus cash benefits paid to those qualified to receive them. With few exceptions, access to cash benefits involves income or means testing. The most important universal program in both countries is the retirement pension ("social security" in the United States and the "state pension" in Britain).

For the households in the lowest fifth of the distribution, income after tax more than doubled as a result of income tax and cash transfers. For the second lowest fifth of the distribution, disposable income exceeded original income in the UK by 64 percent and in the US by 45 percent. For the 20 percent of households in the middle of the distribution, the tax and transfer effect for the two countries calculates to almost the same: disposable income 10 percent above original income. For the fourth and fifth (highest) income groups, the slightly greater progressiveness of the UK income tax is seen, though the difference was not great. The disposable income of the US richest 20 percent fell to 77 percent of original income compared to 75 percent in the UK.

Progressive taxation and cash transfers from government to households had a substantial redistributive effect in both the United States and the United Kingdom. However, statistics from the UK indicate the far greater impact of universal programs for which there are no comparable numbers for the US. Figure 3.3 shows UK

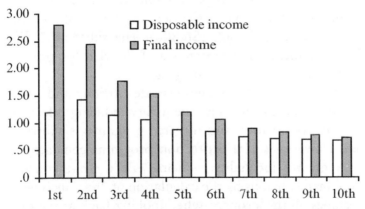

*Figure 3.3 Ratio of disposable income and final income to original income, United Kingdom, by deciles, 2016/17*

Note: Final income is disposable income (see figure 3.2) plus publicly funded benefits in kind, the two most important being primary and secondary schooling and the National Health Service. Source: Office for National Statistics.

household incomes, now in more detail by deciles, for fiscal (tax) year 2016/17. As in the previous figure, we have the ratio of disposal income to original income.

In addition, figure 3.3 shows the ratio of original income to "final income," defined by the UK national statistical organization as disposable income plus programs providing "benefits in kind." The two largest of these programs were the National Health Service (62 percent of benefits in kind) and state-funded schooling (34 percent). In-kind benefits were imputed to each decile group on the basis of estimation of actual use.

A glance at the figure shows the extraordinary distributional impact of the universal programs, which almost triple the income of the poorest 10 percent while having a quite small relative impact at the other end of the distribution. The second-lowest decile had the highest benefits in kind per household – almost £9,000 (about $11,000) – while the richest 10 percent had the lowest total, at £5,600 ($6,800). The substantial difference indicates the preference of the rich for private health care and private schooling.

Figures 2.2 and 2.3 demonstrate obvious and non-obvious conclusions. The inequality-reducing effect of progressive taxation and targeted programs is substantial. Universal social protection programs generate an even greater inequality-reducing effect. That conclusion, made obvious by the calculation of "final income," becomes all the stronger when looking back at the difference between "original income" and "disposable income." It is a universal program, the state pension (Social Security), that provided the largest cash transfer included in disposable income.

## *From Myth to Reality*

Many politicians promote the argument that in recessionary times, when our government's budget falls into deficit (or deeper into deficit), "belt-tightening" becomes necessary or we discover as a country that we "live beyond our means." As explained in the first myth, national governments with their own currencies determine their means themselves, through tax policy and borrowing. The question then arises as to what determines how much a government can spend when it sets its own means. A disarmingly obvious answer presents itself – the collective judgment of the electorate determines what a democratic government should spend.

This book focuses on advanced countries with developed market economies. The constraints on public spending in middle- and, especially, low-income countries with large rural populations lie beyond its scope. Among the advanced countries, levels of income vary substantially. For example, at the end of the 2010s in the European Union, Romania's income per head barely reached $11,000, less than a fifth of Denmark's. With notable exceptions (the United States) the share of public expenditure in GDP rises with the level of development and income per head.

To a great extent this relationship reflects the capacity to tax. In richer countries almost everyone is an employee and almost all production comes from corporate business and government itself, both easily covered by tax collection. Collecting taxes in low-income countries is problematical because of the large portion of self-employed. These structural characteristics of countries provide the context for the collective judgment of the electorate on how much to tax and spend.

Within structural constraints of level of development, in a democracy the representatives elected by the citizenry determine the level, quality and coverage of social services. Public-sector provision of those services provides a powerful vehicle to counter the unequal and discriminatory provision characteristic of private markets. A political decision to reduce public services does not reduce the need for those services in society as a whole. Reducing public services results in a loss of access by households with low incomes, which lack the income to purchase the same or similar services from private providers.

Be it elderly care, health provision, educating adults and children, or transporting people, reduction in social expenditures "saves money" while canceling that monetary saving through the form of lower health of citizens, a less educated population, and lower geographic mobility. Indeed, in the longer term, "saving money" by reducing a preventative service may create the need for greater future expenditure.

In a kind and equitable society, few citizens would object to market provision – what economists call "price rationing" – of hotel rooms and restaurant meals. These are services that, if forgone, have limited impact on basic human welfare. A low income may dictate the decision to shop in a supermarket and eat at home. It is the type of decision all but the richest regularly make. However, in a hypothetical kind and equitable society, the vast majority of citizens would recoil from creating circumstances in which any, much less many, households must choose between food on the table and life-preserving medicine.

Societies do not confront an affordability problem when they have to tighten their belts. Citizens do not face a choice of whether they can as a society afford a social service. The question all citizens face is deciding what kind of society to build and maintain and the policies to achieve it. Print journalists and their counterparts on radio, television and web-based news sources interview public officials and politicians about their expenditure plans for social programs. Almost without exception, in the interview the journalist will hit the politician with the killer question: "How will we pay for that?"

That is the wrong question. The correct question is, "*Should* we pay for that?" If the answer is "yes," governments will find the means to pay. Occasionally societies face the need to "tighten their belt." When they do so, it should be to achieve a noble purpose such as saving our planet from environmental destruction, not to shirk from the commitment to a just society.

# 4

# Never Go into Debt

## *The Myth Itself*

Anxieties about accumulating debts plague the majority of households. Citizens frequently project these anxieties onto governments, a fallacy deconstructed in chapter 1 ("We must live within our means"). That chapter focused almost entirely on public-sector debt. We can now expand the analysis to the debt myth in general. Almost everyone would agree that circumstances arise when going into debt becomes unavoidable. Most would accept that, within closely monitored limits, contracting debt may prove a wise decision. Nonetheless, debt anxiety remains deeply embedded in the mythology of household, business and government budgeting.

In its most generally accepted manifestation, debt anxiety takes the form of a stark warning – under the best of circumstances accumulating debt creates vulnerability to the unforeseen economic dangers inherent in uncertain times – the future is unpredictable and accumulating debt courts disaster. Thus the wise householder, business or government avoids debt to prevent self-inflicted disaster. Concrete evidence of this wise counsel appears with alarming frequency.

Anyone who follows media reports repeatedly learns that economic disasters suffered by households, business and governments are almost without exception associated with unmanageable debt leading to bankruptcy. No household, business or government that made ends meet and avoided debt ever suffered bankruptcy. That is a myth. Debt anxiety has its causality confused. The unfolding of disasters has three aspects: cause, trigger mechanism and how it manifests itself. To take a non-financial example, the common cold results from a virus. A moment of reduced resistance provides the impetus – the trigger – that activates the latent virus. The cold itself takes the form of an above normal temperature.

Similarly, bankruptcy is by definition a collapse under the burden of debt. That is the form it takes, not the cause and not the trigger mechanism. In order to understand the role of debt in bankruptcy we must investigate cause and impetus that turns healthy household, business or government finances into an unmanageable problem that threatens disaster.

Our purpose is to understand why some debt accumulation results in disaster but most does not. According to statistics from the Organisation for Economic Co-operation and Development (OECD), in 2007 France and Poland carried public debts of over 70 percent of gross domestic product (75 and 78 percent, respectively). Japan's public debt to GDP ratio stood at the apparently astronomical 155 percent. In the same year the figures for Ireland and Spain were 28 and 42 percent. Ireland and Spain suffered "sovereign debt" crises that threatened bankruptcy, but France, Poland and Japan did not. There appears to be more to bankruptcy than debt.

Oliver Goldsmith's famous 1770 poem "The Deserted Village" laments the decline of rural society as capitalism developed in the British Isles. Lines 52 and 53 read: "Ill fares the land, to hastening ills a prey, / Where wealth accumulates, and men decay." The debt myth is succinctly stated by substituting "debt" for "wealth."

## Why Debt Accumulates

Because the comparison of public budgets to household budgets is so common, I begin with why households borrow. Investigation of the motivation for borrowing provides a useful start to analyze whether and when indebtedness does or does not become a problem. The reasons for taking on debt vary by type of borrower and the circumstances in which they take on debt. As I have done before, I divide borrowers among households, businesses and governments. All discussion of debt should specify the context, because the organization of finance and the laws governing finance vary across countries. For consistency, our analysis is restricted, as it has been throughout, to advanced market societies with sophisticated, perhaps too sophisticated, financial systems.

Even for the countries with the most developed financial systems cross-country comparisons carry severe limitations due to national practices and values. For example, ease of access to mortgage loans varies considerably among countries. Despite the globalization of credit card use, the institutional forms of consumer debt not linked to an asset vary substantially among countries. For example, in 2014, bank overdrafts and loans from banks and other sources made up 28 percent of British household debt. Credit card debt accounted for only 7.7 percent. In the United States bank borrowing, frequently on the value of dwellings ("home equity") was less important, at 13 percent of non-mortgage debt, with credit card outstanding balances much higher, at 18 percent.

The heavy share of debts incurred for education stands out as one of the striking similarities between the United Kingdom and the United States in recent years. In 2014 outstanding loans incurred for post-secondary education accounted for 31 percent of US non-mortgage household debt. In the early 2010s UK university tuition fees increased astronomically, from about £3,000 a year to over £9,000. In the absence of systemic financial support, this form of personal indebtedness skyrocketed. In 2014 it rose to over 50 percent of UK non-mortgage debt.

Conventional wisdom defines education loans as creating an asset – "investing in your child's education." This putative asset has unique and very limited financial characteristics. If a household falls into dire straits it might sell its automobile or dwelling, but it cannot sell the education asset, which is not a commodity. It is embodied in the educated person. Only the flow of work enhanced by education is saleable, with the sale contingent on market demand. Whether or not the common saying is correct that "education is a good investment," if that investment involves borrowing, the loan remains unsecured.

Whether a debt is secured – balanced by a vendible

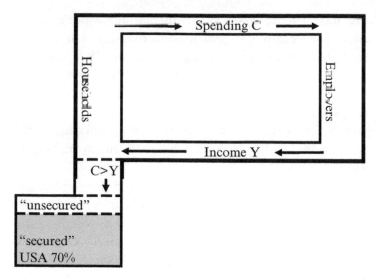

*Figure 4.1 Household income, expenditure and debt*

asset – plays a central role in all indebtedness, as does the distinction between stocks and flows. For all types of lenders and borrowers, households, businesses and governments, income and expenditure are flows and debt is a stock that results from the balance between the two. While that may seem obvious, confusion between flow and stock occurs with alarming frequency. Figure 4.1 demonstrates the stock-flow interaction for households in the simple case of directly earned income – i.e., it assumes no rentier income from property or financial assets. Employers (on the right) pay wages and salaries to working members of households (on the left). If expenditure exceeds income (C, for consumption, greater than Y for income), debt accumulates. The balance between these two flows determines whether debt, the stock, increases or decreases.

As suggested above, private debt falls into two categories: "secured" debt, which the household contracts to purchase an asset such as a home or an automobile; and "unsecured" debt, which has no associated asset. In the United States in 2014 (latest numbers) about 70 percent of household debt fell into the secured category, almost all in mortgages (this and all subsequent statistics come from United States Census Bureau, *Wealth, Asset Ownership and Debt of Households, Detailed Tables: 2014*). Dividing US households into quintiles (fifths), we find that the poorest (lowest) quintile was considerably more likely to hold unsecured debt than secured debt; 22 percent of the poorest households held asset secured debt compared to 78 percent for the richest fifth. Therein lies a message. While the rich can act recklessly (or at least fecklessly) when borrowing, the poor and near-poor must take care against risky credit ventures.

Figure 4.1 helps clarify the effect of economy-wide price changes on debtors and creditors. A rise in prices – inflation – has a different impact on income flow and the stock of secured and unsecured debt. In the private economy, the price of a good or service equals employee incomes, profits, rent, interest and intermediate costs (non-human inputs such as steel in the production of autos). The first four go to households (except for undistributed corporate profit) or to governments as taxes. Intermediate costs, the last, at each stage divide among the same income categories, with the result that, when pursued, prices reduce to income payments.

For that reason the national production of a country equals the sum of all income payments. That equality, which means that national production resolves to the income flows linked to creating the value of that production, has a profound and extremely important implication. When prices rise, the incomes of employees and employers rise. When all prices rise, the incomes of employees and employers rise in the same proportion. Inflation itself does not reduce the real income or purchasing power of the population as a whole.

Were it the case that the general rise in prices went equally to every income recipient across all sectors of the economy, both public and private, inflation would have a neutral effect. A general rise in prices of 5 percent would raise all incomes by 5 percent. Of course, actual price increases never generate this benign neutrality. The reality of inflation, a general rise in prices, is that some prices rise more than others, and some may even go down. The term "general rise in prices" gives a more accurate message than the shorter "inflation." The ubiquitous use of "inflation" for a complex phenomenon tends to foster the fallacious impression of a simple undifferentiated process.

For current purposes, let us consider the simple, undifferentiated case in which a general increase in prices raises everyone's income by the same proportion. Thus, 5 percent inflation implies a 5 percent increase in incomes, leaving purchasing power of all households unchanged. While the inflation in this simple story has no impact on the flows of income and spending (both increase by 5 percent), the debt stock does change. The price-adjusted ("real") value of the accumulated debts falls, by 5 percent. Mortgage holders know this phenomenon quite well. In about 1990 I contracted for a mortgage whose monthly debt service payments calculated at about 20 percent of our household income. Because I had one of those old-fashioned fixed-rate mortgages with unchanging monthly payments, thirty years later the monthly debt service fell to almost half that percentage because of rises in our household income, a substantial part of which resulted from inflation.

This story conveys several generalizations about income and household debt. Inflation makes debt easier for households to service because their money incomes rise while the value of their past debts do not. For the holder of asset-linked debt there is a second benefit – the inflationary increase in the market value of the asset. The cliché that inflation is good for debtors and bad for creditors holds true across the income distribution. For richer households we can double that cliché, because inflation devalues their debt stock and appreciates their asset stock.

Flows and stocks help answer why households borrow. The richer a household is, the more likely it is to borrow to purchase an asset. The assets of all but the very rich are owner-occupied homes and automobiles. With few exceptions, automobiles do not appreciate and homes do. The extent to which a household can gain from the appreciation of dwellings they own is limited. If the dwelling is sold, a replacement must be purchased or the household is left to rent. If the appreciation is general across the housing market, little is gained by sale and repurchase unless the family "down-sizes" or moves to a less expensive area. On balance across households, down-sizing and moving to less expensive areas balance out – little or no net gain.

Changes in financial regulations in the United States produced a mechanism that appeared to give all home owners a method of gaining from the appreciation of dwellings, "home equity loan." As a household slowly pays off its mortgage, a growing portion of the purchase price becomes equity for the household. If simultaneously the market price of the dwelling rises, the difference between the potential sale price and the outstanding mortgage grows. "Equity" embodied in the dwelling rises, which increases the amount that the household can borrow. Some commentators, including a friend of mine who helped write the US legislation facilitating it, hailed this type of borrowing as a democratization of finance. It allegedly gave the majority of American households the ability to benefit from housing market trends without having to realize the value of their property by selling. People could have their house and borrow on it, too.

Home equity as a vehicle to realize wealth suffered from a fatal flaw that revealed the limited "democracy" of finance. The wealthy take advantage of asset appreciation by actually buying and selling the assets. The "equity wealth" of home owners, over 60 percent of American households in 2018, was quite different. Rather than being realized through an actual sale, the borrowed funds derived from the putative, not realized, value of dwellings. The potential or imputed sales value derived from local market conditions, which could change substantially.

In buoyant times, with sales prices high, home ownership seemed the much clichéd "cash cow" for the vast majority of households. The global crash revealed the fragility of borrowing on imputed value. In 2005 about 532,000 home owners received foreclosure notices from their creditors, well less than 1 percent of mortgaged properties. In 2008 the number rose to 2.3 million, and during 2009–10 it hit its peak, at 2.9 million. As late as mid-2018 almost 10 percent of mortgaged properties carried loans at least 25 percent above estimated sales value (numbers from ATTOM Data Solutions online news service and the *World Property Journal* online).

Homes generate a flow of services that replace expenditure on rent. Attempting to use them as a source of income or cash wealth clearly demonstrates the danger of the vast majority seeking to emulate the wealthy few and gain through speculation in financial and housing markets. Over 150 years ago Karl Marx pointed out that everything bought and sold has a dual nature. It has value in use and value in exchange. When an owner-occupier seeks to realize the exchange value of a dwelling while maintaining the use value, potential disaster looms large.

The vast majority of households do not come to the end of the month or year with unspent cash income. That outcome, ending the year with unspent income, remains an experience enjoyed by very few, a fact of life verified by statistics from the United States, Europe and Japan. Indeed, statistics indicate that, in many countries, notably the United Kingdom and the United States, the richest 10 percent of the distribution generate almost all income flow saving. I make the qualification "income flow" because the definition of saving in national statistics varies across countries.

US social security contributions provide an obvious example. These mandatory "contributions" have a dual character. By the usual technical definition of saving as "non-spending," they qualify as implicit saving, a nest egg for retirement, but do not represent an income surplus that a household might choose to spend. To a lesser degree the same applies to many private pension funds that carry penalties for withdrawing money prior to a specified retirement age.

The equity component of mortgage payments should be and in some countries is treated as an imputed form of saving. This part of the monthly mortgage bill accumulates as equity if market conditions do not undermine the sales value of the dwelling. These implicit and imputed forms of saving indicate the complex nature of the cliché "barely living within your means." A household well up the income distribution but still far from the top 1 percent may come to the end of the year with no surplus income – all earnings spent, much of it on discretionary purchases and a small part in accumulating equity. The household at the bottom of the distribution that rents accommodation and has no private pension finds itself in quite a different case of "barely living within its means."

All but the richest households have a common characteristic, though some struggle to "make ends meet" and others do not. A clear explanation of what separates the 1 percent from those of us in the 99 percent comes from an unexpected source, a 1980s Carl Barks cartoon featuring Donald Duck and Scrooge McDuck. For those unfamiliar with this cartoon series, Scrooge McDuck is the world's richest duck and Donald his working-class nephew (employed by Scrooge and foster parent to three nephews of his own, Huey, Dewey and Louie). At the outset of the cartoon, on a Friday Donald collects his salary check from the paymaster of McDuck Enterprises, which he changes to cash at a nearby branch of the First McDuck Bank. With the cash he fills his car with fuel (bought at a McDuck Service Station), purchases his weekly food (at a McDuck Supermarket), and pays his rent (at the offices of McDuck Property Management).

Having made these expenditures, Donald finds himself out of funds ("broke"). He goes to his uncle and requests an advance on his pay for the coming week. Scrooge eyes him critically and tells Donald that he cannot manage his money, ending with the punchline "You never find me broke at the end of the week."

The cartoon carries a deep message, succinctly summarized by the distinguished Polish economist Michał Kalecki in the phrase "workers spend what they get and capitalists get what they spend," repeated and incorporated into a famous economic model by the British economist Nicholas Kaldor. The vast majority of adults work for someone else. Each working day they sell their capacity to work. They receive their pay and spend almost all of it, which necessitates that they repeat the work–spend cycle indefinitely.

In contrast, the private employer spends on the elements necessary to produce a good or service which he or she sells. If the sale price doesn't cover costs, the employer soon joins the 99 percent as an employee. The successful employer recovers costs plus a profit. Subject to market conditions, employers garner profit in proportion to how much they spend. Thus, the 99 percent spend what they get and the 1 percent gets what it spends. This basic difference between the employee and employer explains the relationship to debt of the two household groups, the 99 percent and the 1 percent.

The vast majority of households borrow in order to cover necessary expenditures if they are poor or to purchase durable commodities that generate a flow of services to replace direct purchase – home ownership instead of renting, a washing machine instead of paying a laundromat, and a private vehicle instead of public transport. Neither type of borrowing generates the cash flow to pay for the service on the debt stock that the borrowing creates. That must be done from existing income flow. Some households in the 99 percent may partially service their debt through cash income vehicles such as Airbnb and less ubiquitous schemes for private automobiles. Only a few can delve into this so-called sharing economy because the flexibility not to use the dwelling and the automobile is the necessary precondition. The businessperson faces no such constraint.

Production for sale drives business borrowing, with established enterprises finding it much easier to increase their borrowing and scale of production than "start-ups." Commercial banks have quite good reason to prefer lending to established companies. In the United States the Small Business Administration reported that, during 2010–15, half of start-ups lasted at least five years, but the number of annual closures exceeded that of start-ups, implying a slight decline in the total number of small businesses. The relative caution of commercial lenders towards business shows in "delinquency" rates on outstanding loans.

Figure 4.2 reports the share of three types of loan by US commercial banks which were one month or more in arrears for the twenty years 1998 to 2017. For all years, credit card arrears have the highest delinquent rates, reaching almost 7 percent during the global financial crisis and an average of 3.9 percent for the twenty years. Other consumer loans, which include some for durable goods, show the next highest rates (average 3.1 percent), followed, much lower, by all loans for busi-

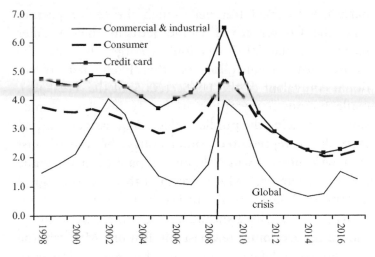

*Figure 4.2* "*Delinquent*" *loans of US commercial banks by type, 1998–2017 (percentage of loans of each type)*

Note: "Delinquent" is defined as one month or more overdue.
Source: Federal Reserve Bank of St Louis.

ness purposes, commercial and industrial enterprises (1.9 percent).

The figure conveys an important relationship that needs further inspection: the interaction of indebtedness and fluctuations of the economies in which those debts are embedded. Analyzing that relationship leads to insights about public indebtedness that complement the extensive discussion in chapters 1 and 2 that explained the "balancing" role of public expenditure.

### Debt and the Economic Cycle

The UK election of May 2010 brought to government a coalition of the Liberal Democrat and Conservative parties, with the latter very much the senior partner (and the Conservatives would jettison their smaller partner for the 2015 election). George Osborne, the Conservative Chancellor of the Exchequer (functional equivalent of the US Secretary of the Treasury), made famous a metaphor to justify his dogged pursuit of balancing the public budget. Aggressively cutting expenditure represented sound policy, he argued, just as a wise home owner should "repair the roof while the sun is shining." Many accepted this meteorological metaphor. A leaky roof can result in severe structural damage to a dwelling should a storm come. By analogy, should an economic tempest hit Britain, Mr Osborne maintained, a deficit in the public budget and the associated increasing indebtedness would damage faith in government and the stability of society.

While this may seem common sense, it qualifies as flat-earth thinking that households and businesses reject in practice. Were it true, in prosperous times households and businesses would pay down their debts. The opposite occurs. During prosperous times households and businesses accumulate debt. When prosperity ends, debt repayment begins.

Empirical evidence helps us understand why businesses and households would behave in this way. Figure 4.3 provides the debt version of the economic balancing explained in chapters 1 and 2, demonstrated there with some simple graphics using the metaphor of a scale. Figure 4.3 shows the outstanding debt of US households, non-financial businesses and the federal government over eighteen years, 2000–17. I exclude financial corporations because they represent the primary source of lending to private debtors. To facilitate comparison I

# Never Go into Debt

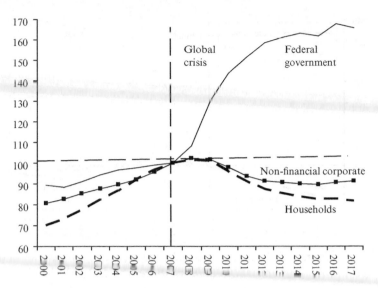

*Figure 4.3 United States: federal, non-financial corporate, and household debt as share of GDP (2007 =100)*

*Note:* The figures for GDP at the end of 2017 were: federal 103 percent, non-financial corporate 151 percent, and household 80 percent.

*Source:* Federal Reserve Bank of St Louis.

have set each category of debt to 100 in 2007, the year before the global crisis (the debt to GDP ratios for 2017 appear in the note).

In the expansionary years 2000–7, all three categories increased debts, with government liabilities increasing the least. US households and businesses show similar movement, accumulating debt as the economy expanded during that time, then reducing the debt share in GDP in the years after the crisis. Towards the end of the 2010s, business debt levels off and begins to increase again. In total contrast, public debt rises at an accelerating rate through 2012, when it continues to increase, but at a

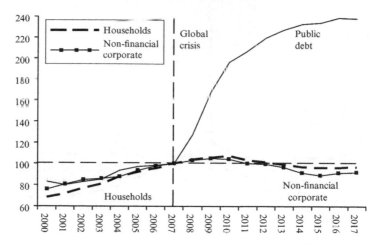

*Figure 4.4  United Kingdom: federal, non-financial corporate, and household debt as share of GDP (2007 =100)*

Note: The figures for GDP at the end of 2017 were: public 88 percent, non-financial corporate 168 percent, and household 86 percent.
Source: Federal Reserve Bank of St Louis.

slower rate, and reaches a peak in 2016 to slightly over 100 percent of GDP.

Before attempting an explanation of the US pattern, the same diagram for the United Kingdom warrants a look (figure 4.4), and the similarity of the two is so great that they appear clones of each other. Public debt shows the only substantial difference, with the proportion increase in the UK considerably greater than that in the United States. What both figures reveal is that businesses and households accumulate debt in good times and pay it down in recessions. Any other result would be absurd. Servicing a growing debt requires a growing income. Incomes grow during expansion and decline during recession.

122

# Never Go into Debt

What if governments followed the example of businesses and households, paying off debts in recessionary times and increasing them in expansionary periods? That pattern of borrowing and repaying courts disaster. Economies expand because government, household and export spending induces businesses to increase their productive capacity to meet the growing demand. The fact of households paying off debts implies spending less on goods and services. Less spending on goods and services means that the expansion does not occur. No rational business management would increase capacity when demand falls and sales flounder.

If the government follows the practice of the household, we have a systemic tendency to economic stagnation – households paying off debt instead of purchasing goods and services, which discourages private investment, reinforced by government reducing debt instead of spending. Prudence by households and government may seem commendable in the abstract, but in practice it is the economics of the madhouse – behavior that generates a continually depressed economy. To fight recession, governments should behave in the opposite way to debt-reducing businesses and households – spend when its private-sector counterparts do not spend.

Germany provides an excellent example of the consequences if the macroeconomic policy of a national government mimics household behavior. In Germany, avoiding debt is described as behaving like a Swabian housewife, referring to a region in the southwest of the country (one is left to speculate on the budgetary prudence or otherwise of the Swabian *Hausherr*). For various conjunctural reasons, including the unification

123

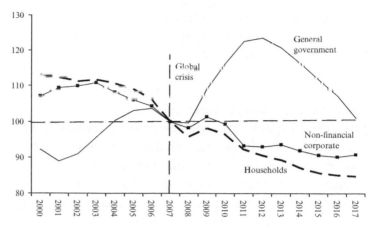

*Figure 4.5 Germany: all government, non-financial corporate, and household debt as a share of GDP (2007 =100)*

Note: The figures for GDP at the end of 2017 were: general government 65 percent, non-financial corporate 105 percent, and household 53 percent.
Source: Federal Reserve Bank of St Louis.

of the country in 1989, after creation of the eurozone, German governments pursued budget surpluses with single-minded focus.

Figure 4.5 shows the Swabian housewife behavior of German business, households and central government. During the relatively prosperous years immediately before the global crisis, German businesses and households engaged in paying off their debts while the public debt grew slightly. Following an initial economic recovery driven by public borrowing during 2008–10, in 2012 the German government took the advice of the eponymous *Hausfrau* of Swabia, running budget surpluses and reducing the debt to GDP ratio. Households did the same, reducing their debts, as did business.

During the seventeen years 2001–17, the German economy expanded at an average annual rate of 1.2 percent. The other eighteen eurozone countries averaged 2 percent and the nine non-euro EU members 2.5 percent. The meager growth of the debt-reducing, budget-surplus-burdened German economy resulted from exports, which expanded from 2010 at the relatively modest rate of 3.7 percent, slower than the average for the other eighteen eurozone countries and lower than for the nine non-euro economies (all statistics from Eurostat). After the global crisis, many commentators and politicians cited Germany as the motor of the European economy, an engine of growth and export success on account of its Swabian prudence, manifest in sound budget surpluses.

The truth is quite different. During the latter part of the 2010s, German policy functioned as a drag on the expansion of the European economy. That drag carried a clear message. If all major economic groups increase their saving, paying down their debts, they all stagnate together.

Is debt a bad thing? It is for those debtors who cannot service their outstanding loans. Far worse than a minority taking on unmanageable debt is the majority paying theirs down. If some spend less than their incomes, others must spend more than theirs. It really is that simple.

## Myth and Reality

Living within our means yields a frequently repeated warning about debt, for households, businesses and governments. As much as we might wish to believe otherwise, we cannot "grow out of debt." Nor can debt be carried indefinitely. At some point the debt chickens come home to roost, demanding payment. Closely related comes the reminder that governments, like households, cannot spend their way out of debt.

Actually, governments can and have on many occasions spent their way out of debt. Extraordinary events, usually wars and global turbulence, leave governments with no choice but to accumulate extraordinary levels of debt. Figure 4.6 shows the public debt history of the United Kingdom and the United States over more than a century (1900–2016). During the twentieth century both governments fought two major wars and suffered through the major international depression of the 1930s.

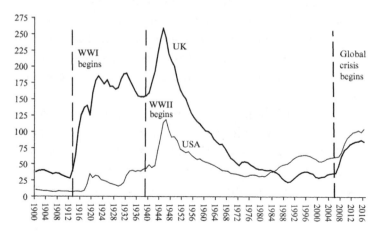

*Figure 4.6 Governments grow out of debt: debt to GDP ratio for the United Kingdom and the United States, 1900–2016*

Note: For both countries the debt is for central government; levels are not strictly comparable because of country-specific definitions.
Source: Bank of England, *A Millennium of Macroeconomic Data* (2018) and www.usgovernmentspending.com/.

# Never Go into Debt

Few if any would accuse a government of irresponsible budgeting when it borrows to finance a war that threatens the existence of the country, as was the case with both world wars. The British government financed both wars through borrowing. At the beginning of "The Great War" in 1914, the UK public debt to GDP stood at 64 percent compared to that in the US at 8 percent. Smaller but still substantial wars in the previous twenty years, plus gathering tensions among European governments, explain the size of the British government debt compared to that of the relatively isolated and isolationist American government. By the end of the war the public debt had risen well above 100 percent of GDP.

Throughout the 1920s and 1930s the British government implemented a version of austerity, attempting to achieve balanced budgets. In every year from 1920 to 1938 the UK government ran an overall surplus (statistics from Bank of England millennial tables). These constrained budgets, and a dysfunctional attempt to maintain the link between the pound and gold resulted in unstable growth rates throughout the interwar years. In the United States the Roosevelt administration had considerably better success using a budgetary stimulus to generate recovery from the Great Depression (though unwisely cut back spending in 1938, which temporarily arrested growth).

The World War II debt numbers jump from the figure. In the United States public debt increased exponentially after 1940, from 43 percent of GDP in 1939 to almost 120 percent just seven years later. The timing of the UK increase was the same, though at a much higher level, from 156 percent of GDP in 1939 to 256 percent in 1946. As the war came to an end, the governments of both countries seemed mired in debt far above any previous level. If ever public debt would undermine prosperity, the immediate post-war years seem prime candidates for seeing this happen.

Quite the opposite occurred. The average annual rate of expansion of the UK economy during the first ten years after World War II ended exceeded 3 percent and averaged 5 percent in the 1950s. As result, the public debt "burden," 200 percent of GDP in 1949, fell to 107 percent in 1959 and to a modest 60 percent in 1969. None of this decline in debt to GDP resulted from reducing the debt itself – in 1969 the UK public debt was 17 percent larger than in 1946. Though less dramatic in degree of debt reduction, the US story was the same, GDP expanding at an average rate of 3.9 percent in the 1950s and an even more impressive 4.7 percent in the 1960s. The debt to GDP ratio fell from 93 percent in 1949, to 55 percent in 1959, and below 40 percent by 1969.

Consider by comparison the attempt to bring down the Greek debt to GDP ratio through austerity policies. After considerable negotiation in 2012, the Greek government applied the strict budget austerity program designed by the so-called Troika (the European Commission, the European Central Bank and the International Monetary Fund). When the program began, the EU measure of the public debt was 160 percent of GDP. After five years of austerity designed to reduce that ratio, at the end of 2017 debt had risen to 176 percent of GDP. The size of the economy had declined as a result of the demand-reducing public expenditure cuts and the debt in euros had increased because negative growth meant lower tax revenues. Far from reducing debt, expenditure cuts caused GDP and tax revenue to fall, prolonging the need for the Greek government to borrow.

Growing out of debt is more than possible. It represents the only successful policy for debt reduction. In order to stimulate debt-reducing growth, a government may need to increase its budget deficit and, thus, its debt. That may seem absurd: decrease debt by first increasing it. Nonetheless, it leads to successful debt reduction for governments, while attempting to generate a budget surplus through expenditure reduction does not.

This rule of debt reduction applies equally to business and households – income growth, not "belt-tightening," is the most effective and fastest route to sustainable debt. Private income growth occurs when the economy as a whole makes the transition from recession to expansion. A purposeful economic stimulus from the public budget brings about that transition through its demand-generating impact.

From the myth of "never go into debt" we come to the reality of sound budgeting. When governments use their budgets to maintain stability and expansion for the economy as a whole, everyone gains. When private-sector demand falters, stability and expansion require governments to take the lead. It is a benign circle in which all benefit.

# 5

# Taxes Are a Burden

## *The Myth Itself*

I begin by stating the anti-tax argument in its clearest form – tax reduces people's ability to spend.

People's incomes come from their work and, for a wealthy few, property income supplements or may exceed earnings from wages and salaries. Because both public and private pensions link to work, the same applies to the retired. In a market economy people sustain themselves, frugally or lavishly, by spending their income. By definition, when income falls, the means to sustain one's self also falls.

Taxes reduce take-home pay, as every employee knows well. On the monthly pay slip we find two income flows stated: gross pay before taxes and net pay after tax. The difference between the two is lost consumption. A full-time employed person who pays 20 percent of gross pay in tax in effect works for forty weeks to earn income and ten weeks for the government (assuming two weeks' holiday). For a 250-day working year, that person works the first fifty days for the government.

Taxes are a burden, carried reluctantly. Some taxation cannot be avoided, and the lower the tax payments, the freer is the working person to achieve the goal of personal and family fulfillment. The income governments demand from those they govern reduces personal freedom.

Lest a reader think I make this up, this condemnation of taxation appears in a US organization named the Tax Foundation in its proposal for "Tax Freedom Day." Tax Freedom Day is a significant date for taxpayers and lawmakers because it represents how long Americans as a whole have to work in order to pay the nation's tax burden. On its website, the Tax Foundation elaborates:

> This year [2018], Americans again will work the longest to pay federal, state, and local individual income taxes (44 days). Payroll taxes will take 26 days to pay, followed by sales and excise taxes (15 days), corporate income taxes (seven days), and property taxes (11 days). The remaining six days are spent paying estate and inheritance taxes, customs duties, and other taxes.

Few would agree with this extreme view of the revenue function of governments, but many would embrace the milder version, that governments should tax as little as possible – if not the bare minimum, then close to it. Some activities individuals cannot fund and organize themselves. Most of these are services, such as fire-fighting and national defense. A fire department that serves only those who have paid cannot do its job. A national defense system must protect the entire territory of a country. Social scientists name such activities

131

"public goods," defined as a good or a service that can exclude no one if it functions effectively.

With public goods in mind, the pure "taxes are a burden" ideology changes to a more superficially reasonable argument – taxes burden us to the extent that governments impose them to fund activities that the private sector could supply. Just as a cobbler should stick to the last, governments should limit themselves to public goods. When government do not so restrict themselves, tax becomes a burden.

This version of the burden argument, tax to supply public goods, suffers from the same basic failing as the overly ideological one. Both and all "tax is a burden" arguments treat people as isolated individuals rather than as members of an interactive and ongoing society. Because people are members of society, the "tax is a burden" argument is false. It is a myth.

### The Eponymous Taxpayer

All discussions of public expenditure at some point refer to the "taxpayer." One presumes that the meaning of the word is "he, she or it that pays taxes." In practice it carries portentous implications: a person who bears the cost of public spending. Far from being merely descriptive, the term "taxpayer" weighs into discussions of public policy laden with ideological baggage. Latent in the use of the word lies the implied division between those who pay their tax and "pull their weight" and those who shirk and enjoy a free ride. "Taxpayer" represents a key polemical term providing support for the austerity doctrine – all public spending proposals, no matter how beneficial they may appear, must be borne by and become a burden on the "taxpayer."

The shirkers living off the taxpayer are not always the feckless welfare recipients. The Bush administration recapitalized potentially bankrupt financial corpora-tions in 2008 through the Troubled Asset Relief Program (TARP) that authorized $700 billion, followed two years later by the Wall Street Reform and Consumer Protection Act. The media frequently referred to the recapitalization as "taxpayer bailouts." Critics on both the left and right denounced TARP and demanded "bailout Main Street, not Wall Street," calling for help to small business and home owners rather than the big New York ("Wall Street") banks.

The business magazine *Forbes*, famous for its annual list of billionaires, in July 2015 told its readers that "The new financial tools were backed by the govern-ment so that taxpayers would get hung with the bill." However one might assess the wisdom of the financial recapitalizations in the United States and Europe, they do not qualify as "taxpayer bailouts." The funds for the "bailouts" did not come from taxation. The "bailees" received their funds from the US Treasury via the pur-chase of "non-performing assets" – bad loans. Far from costing tax money, the US Treasury more than fully recaptured the recapitalization funds, recovering $441 billion on an outlay of $426 billion, for a $15 billion profit. In the United Kingdom the National Audit Office reported in mid-2017 recovery of 95 percent of "bail-out" funds.

A European equivalent of the US and UK taxpayer bailouts came during the sovereign debt crisis suffered by several European governments during 2010–15, especially in Greece. The European media repeated an assertion by the German Ministry of Finance that "German taxpayers" bore the cost of "the bailout of the Greeks," suggesting that the prudent Germans had saved the irresponsible Greeks from economic disaster. In addition to suffering from the error of personifying countries, the assertion is false. The "bailout of Greece" involved the recapitalization of banks located in Greece, most of which were German owned. The German government's contribution to recapitalization of banks in Greece was recycled back to Germany, into the balance sheet of financial institutions.

This rhetoric of taxpayer bailouts indicates the ideological nature of most discussions of taxation, which requires terminological clarity in order to sort the valid from the invalid. As a first step in clarification, note that in most countries the vast majority of public revenue falls into three categories: 1) direct taxes, which are levied on incomes; 2) indirect taxes, levied on transactions (also known as sales taxes, *ad valorem* taxes and value added taxes); and 3) fees and charges on specific activities (automobile license plates and, in the United Kingdom, the "TV license" for the BBC). All three involve taxation of a flow (income), of transactions or of a recurrent activity. Also in the category of direct taxes are those on stocks of value, the most frequent tax on the value of property.

It may seem obvious who pays each type of tax: people pay the personal income tax, corporations pay the corporate income tax, buyers pay sales taxes, and users pay fees. Why then, in assessing the election manifesto of the Labour Party in May 2017, did an economist at the UK Institute for Fiscal Studies (IFS) assert that "all taxes are

# Taxes Are a Burden

paid by people"? This statement carries a quite strong ideological message – whatever the form of the tax, it ends up falling on you and me. Talking about taxing corporations is just talk; it's always people that pay taxes.

From the world of observed phenomena, the IFS assertion takes us into the rather arcane field of "tax incidence." This exercise by public finance experts seeks to identify who or what "bears" the tax, in contrast to who makes an actual payment. Some of the "incidence" analysis conforms to what the non-expert might conclude. We can see from our own behavior that sales taxes reduce the amount of a good or service that we consume. As a result, the supplier of the good or service bears part of the impact of the tax through lower sales, revenue and profit. In some cases – sales of alcoholic beverages and tobacco products are the most obvious – lower sales is the purpose of the sales tax.

The importance of the demand-reducing effect depends on the good or service. In the dead of winter a rise in the cost of heating is unlikely to have much impact on household consumption other than for the very poor. In contrast, a company that hikes up the price of its chocolate bar will likely suffer a rush by chocoholics to alternative sources for their addiction (what economists call "elasticity" of demand, availability of substitutes).

As the layperson would expect, expert opinion assigns the incidence of the personal income tax to the person who pays the tax, though a few argue that employers partly bear the incidence. No such controversy exists about the income tax paid by the self-employed or rentiers. As the quotation from the IFS functionary would suggest, considerable controversy swirls around who

135

pays corporate income tax. The controversy reflects ideology more than economics. The mainstream Tax Policy Center in Washington, DC, and the progressive Tax Justice Network agree that corporate managers and shareholders overwhelmingly bear the corporate income tax, the former estimating their share at 80 percent. That represents the consensus view.

This brief look at the esoteric world of tax incidences allows us to proceed with the following generalizations. People pay the personal income tax and, the more progressive the rates, the greater the inequality reducing effect. People also pay indirect taxes, and these have a regressive impact on distribution. And, finally, because the incomes of corporate managers and shareholders generally fall into the highest income brackets, taxes on corporate profits reduce income inequality.

The word "eponymous," which did not enter my vocabulary until I was well into my forties, means "named after a specific person or group." "Taxpayer" should not be used eponymously. No person exists in any country who epitomizes the attributes of those who pay taxes. Some taxpayers are rich, others poor. Some pay their tax directly (withheld by their employer) and others indirectly (added onto purchases by the seller). Statements such as "the taxpayer bears the cost of bailouts" are in some cases factually wrong and always refer to an invalid collectivity.

## Taxes in the Concrete

Taxes are what we pay our government so it can effectively manage the aggregate economy to carry out the tasks we assign to it through the democratic process. Some of those tasks have a history as long as the nation-state itself, such as defense of the homeland. Many others began towards the end of the ninetenth century (health care in Germany for example), and a few arrived relatively recently (programs focused on environmental protection).

As we search for generalizations, figure 5.1 shows with statistics for twenty countries one of the most obvious. As the average income of citizens rises, so too does each person's tax share. The numbers next to the country names are the percentage of GDP that goes to tax. The figure displays the countries in descending order of income per

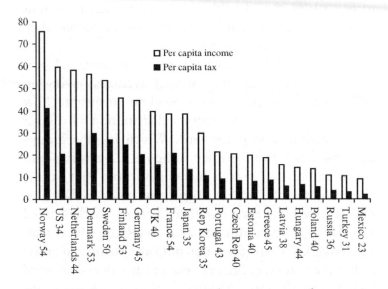

*Figure 5.1 Per capita income and per capita tax for twenty countries, all levels of government, 2017 (US$ thousands)*

Source: World Bank for per capita income and OECD for tax shares.

capita, first ten advanced market economies, then ten more at various points in the transition to join the first ten. In all but two of the richest ten, 40 percent or more of income goes to tax. The United States, at 34 percent, and Japan, at 35 percent, are the low-tax countries.

The numbers raise questions that require closer inspection. We might begin with explaining the relatively low American share. Then how do we explain that, in 2017, Japan and France, with very similar per capita income, had such different tax levels? Or that the French government raised 54 percent of national income in tax and just across the channel the British share was far lower at 40 percent? These numbers seem to convey the message that what people consider an appropriate amount of tax to pay varies considerably across countries. If citizens consider tax a "burden," no consensus exists on when that burden is large or small.

In part the differences we observe in figure 5.1 perplex us because they are national averages, giving no indication of who pays what type of tax. Inspecting how tax is assigned across the income distribution moves our understanding a step forward. Which income groups pay how much tax is shown in figure 5.2 across population quintiles. It may come as a surprise that, in the United States, the richest 20 percent pay a higher portion of total taxes than in either Germany or the United Kingdom – 70 percent compared to 54 and 49 percent. The large US share does not indicate greater equality; rather the contrary. Because the pre-tax distribution of income was the most unequal in the United States, we should expect this result; with a large proportion of household income accruing to the top 20 percent, that quintile pays a greater share of total tax.

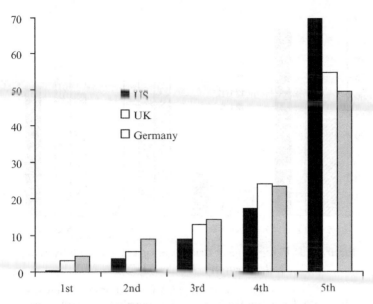

*Figure 5.2 Government taxes on US, UK and German households by income quintile, mid-2010s*

Note: US figures are for 2014 and UK ones for 2015/16.
Source: US Congressional Budget Office and UK Office for National Statistics.

The type of taxes people pay also strongly affects the share of tax across the income distribution. Because the richest 20 percent do almost all the saving in a country, indirect taxes weigh more heavily the lower a household is in the distribution. While indirect taxes account for a quite small share of US public revenue, they contribute substantially in Germany and the United Kingdom – indeed, in all European countries. European Union law requires that every member government levy at least a 15 percent transaction tax ("value added tax" or simply VAT). At the end of the 2010s the UK rate was 20 percent and that in Germany 19 percent.

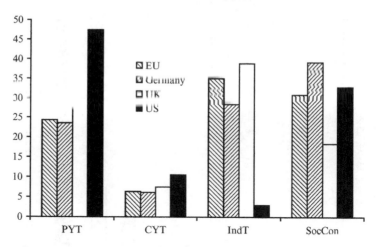

*Figure 5.3 Percentage distribution of tax revenue by type,*
*EU, Germany, UK and US, 2015*

*Note:* PYT = personal income tax; CYT = corporate income tax;
IndT = indirect tax; SocCon = social contributions. Following
convention, I use Y for income rather than I, which is usually
reserved for investment.
*Source:* US, *Economic Report of the President 2018*; EU, *Taxation
Trends in the European Union 2017*.

Figure 5.3 shows differences in tax sources for the
United States and European countries. Government
revenue falls into four categories: personal income tax
(PYT), corporate income tax (CYT), indirect taxes
(IndT) and social contributions (SocCon). The first
three have been discussed previously. The fourth refers
to various taxes on employees and employers formally
assigned to specific expenditures. Almost all governments of advanced market countries fund retirement
programs by taxes "earmarked" for the purpose. The
social security "contributions" (they are compulsory)
represent the most important of these in the US. UK

national insurance "contributions" (again, compulsory) have a similar but not identical function. In all countries covered in figure 5.3 the personal income tax and social contributions are direct taxes because employees and employers pay them. They differ in that personal income tax has a strongly progressive rate structure while social contributions do not.

Most striking is the importance of personal income tax in the United States, bringing in almost half of public revenue (47 percent), compared to 28 percent in the United Kingdom and less than 25 percent in the European Union (slightly less in Germany, the largest EU member). The share of US revenue from taxes on corporate income also exceeds what the others collect, though with a considerably smaller difference. A minuscule share for indirect taxes ("excise taxes" in US terminology) counterbalances the dominance of the personal income tax. The other anomaly in the table, the low UK share for social contributions, results from the British practice of funding the state pension from general revenue rather than a designated levy.

The major role of personal income taxes in the United States has a history coming out of war and progressive political movements. The US Constitution prohibits direct taxes unless the federal government distributes the revenue to states on the basis of population (Article 1, Section 2, Clause 3). Nonetheless, Abraham Lincoln introduced the first federal income tax in 1861, at a flat-rate of 3 percent on individual incomes above $800. In 1862 Congress amended the tax law to make it slightly progressive, while specifying that it would terminate in 1866. If it was meant to continue for the duration of the

Civil War, 1866 proved a good guess (the war formally ended on 10 May 1865).

Throughout the rest of the nineteenth century, progressive groups campaigned for reinstating a federal income tax. This appeared in the Socialist Party platform in 1887 and was adopted by the Populist Party in 1892 and by the mainstream Democratic Party two years later. In response to popular pressure, the Democrat-controlled US Congress passed the Wilson–Gorman Tariff Act (the president was also a Democrat), which included a 2 percent federal levy on incomes over $4,000.

Barely a year later, the US Supreme Court declared this tax on incomes unconstitutional. There followed a push by progressives for a constitutional amendment specifically to legalize income taxes. After a campaign characterized by class divisions, the one-sentence Sixteenth Amendment survived the protracted ratification process: "The Congress shall have power to lay and collect taxes on incomes, from whatever source derived, without apportionment among the several States, and without regard to any census or enumeration."

Born out of an imperative to defend the unity of the United States and added to the US Constitution in one of the most important progressive political victories before Franklin D. Roosevelt became president, the Sixteenth Amendment determined the focus of federal taxation for the following 100 years and more. The UK income tax has a longer history. First introduced, as in the US, to fund a war, against Napoleonic France in 1798, it became a major source of revenue in the twentieth century. But, unlike in the US, taxes on consumption represented a major source of revenue: the "purchase

tax" (introduced in 1940, again a war-prompted measure) was subsumed under the value added tax upon
membership of the European Union in 1973.

Compared to the political struggle for a progressive
income tax, the major source of revenue in the European
Union, VAT, has a singularly dull history. Its design
is usually attributed to separate proposals in the early
1900s by a German businessman, Wilhelm von Siemens
(the same Siemens family as in the infamous Siemens–
Schuckert business group that developed close links to
the Nazi regime), and an American academic, Thomas
Sewall Adams. VAT by its nature weighs more heavily
on lower income groups. It does not tax saving, and in
every country only the rich save. Exemptions for necessities can make it less regressive (as in the UK), though
this is a very blunt policy instrument.

No discussion of tax burdens can avoid considering
the purpose for which a government raises the revenue.
Table 5.1 looks at where three governments actually
spend their revenue. While definitions vary across
countries, the categories in the table have sufficient
consistency to allow useful comparisons. As a practical
matter, two of the categories, general public services
and national security, cover activities every government
must provide. General public services cover funding for
foreign policy, administering the day-to-day activity of
government and mundane activities such as maintaining the national transport system. Since the inception of
the nation-state, governments have spent to secure the
country against threats both foreign and domestic. What
debate occurs over these two universally recognized
functions of government, administration and "defense
of the realm," focuses on efficiency and effectiveness.

Table 5.1 Distribution of central government expenditures, Germany, United Kingdom and United States, 2017 (percentage of total expenditure)

|  | Germany | UK | US |
| --- | --- | --- | --- |
| Pensions & unemployment | 22.1 | 23.2 | 32.2 |
| Social support | 21.3 | 15.8 | 5.6 |
| Health & care | 16.3 | 19.2 | 28.8 |
| Education | 9.8 | 11.6 | 1.8 |
| General public services | 13.5 | 5.0 | 3.9 |
| National security | 5.8 | 7.4 | 15.4 |
| Interest on debt | 1.0 | 6.3 | 5.9 |
| Other* | 10.2 | 11.5 | 4.0 |
| Tax/GDP central govt | 44.4 | 34.4 | 27.1 |

Note: *For UK, includes transfers to local and regional governments and payments to the EU; for Germany, includes 7 percent for "economic affairs."

Source: UK Office for National Statistics; US *Economic Report of the President 2018.*

Differences in categories other than interest payments derive from the political preferences of the citizenry. Direct income payments linked to work, retirement programs and unemployment compensation make up the largest spending category in all three countries. Controversy about this type of spending focuses primarily on the division between public and private funding, not on the justification of the spending itself. The same applies to spending on the health and care of the population and on education. A purely technocratic approach to these expenditures would center on whether the private or the public sector delivers the activity more effectively. For very good reason public debate does not emphasize a technocratic approach.

Except in rare cases, the public and private sectors do not deliver the same product or service, even if superficially that seems the case. As should be obvious, a private company such as Federal Express provides a different delivery service than a national postal system. Less obvious, the postal service itself undergoes a basic reorientation in its relationship to the public when a government decides to privatize it (as in the United Kingdom in 2012). The legislation creating the US postal service explicitly assigned to it facilitating the geographic and social integration of the nation. Authorized in Article I, Section 8, of the US Constitution, public service remains the mission of the Post Office (found in Title 39 of the United States Code):

> The Postal Service shall have as its basic function the obligation to provide postal services to bind the Nation together through the personal, educational, literary, and business correspondence of the people. It shall provide prompt, reliable, and efficient services to patrons in all areas and shall render postal services to all communities.

This emphasis shows itself in more colorful language in the famous but unofficial motto of the letter carrier (chiseled into the stone over the entrance to the central New York City post office on Eighth Avenue in Manhattan): "Neither snow nor rain nor heat nor gloom of night stays these couriers from the swift completion of their appointed rounds." A privatized postal service, such as the British Royal Mail, is unlikely to commit to "bind the nation" and persevere through "gloom of night."

The example of the US postal service leads to a general conclusion. Though commonly used, the term "tax burden" is inappropriate. The taxes raised by governments fund activities that if not done by the public sector would require private funding. They involve a funding obligation in the same sense that households pay rent and buy food. They are essentials for the reproduction of the family and society. The citizens of a country cannot avoid such "burdens." The issue is not reducing a burden but making a political choice between private and public funding, whether the burden falls on the individual or on society.

The final category of public expenditure, interest payments on public debt, remains for inspection. Does the increase in interest mean that public borrowing became a burden? As I have explained, the debt itself does not qualify as a burden. If the public sector could borrow at zero interest and always replace maturing debt with new zero-interest borrowing, no burden exists. We are then in the world of Fred Hoyle and the meteor of gold (see chapter 1). Public debt may be viewed as a burden if it requires repayment and if it involves interest payments to non-government creditors (that is, the interest does not recycle back to the government itself).

The conditional verb used, "may be viewed," is necessary because of the nature of the debt itself and the interest payments to service it. Consider the case of a mortgage, which involves a purchase over time. While people may complain about mortgage payments, they result from a choice by the household of how to fund its shelter. More importantly, they result in ownership of an asset. The decision, public or private, to purchase an asset doesn't create a burden except in the unhappy case in which the asset loses its value. If the asset chosen to purchase yields a return greater than the interest payments, the result is an income gain to the private or public purchasers of the asset.

# Taxes Are a Burden

Whether private or public debt links to an equivalent asset reveals a more fundamental debt reality – every debt contract has a twofold nature. It is an asset for the creditor and a liability for the borrower, a characteristic frequently ignored in discussions of whether debt burdens present and future taxpayers. These alleged burdens go hand in hand, the debt burden doubling up the tax burden. It is bad enough, goes the tax burden narrative, that citizens must bear the dead weight of coercive taxation; that burden becomes unbearable when it involves no pretense of funding a public service but merely services excessive spending of the past.

One aspect of this narrative we dispelled previously. The public debt of national governments can accumulate for sound economic and social causes. The recent large increases in national government debt in the United States and Europe came as the direct result of the global financial crisis at the end of 2000s. This was due partly to the automatic tendency of public revenue to decline in recessions and partly to public expenditures seeking to rebalance the economy by replacing the collapse of private investment.

Even if the accumulation of public debt has a functional explanation, might it still be a burden on current and future generations to service and repay? The answer is "no." First, the meaning of "repay" requires clarification. National governments continuously repay their debts. For example, the US government issues Treasury notes (T-notes for short) in denominations of $1,000 with maturity dates of two to ten years. If one buys a $1,000 two-year T-note with a 3 percent interest rate on January 1, the Treasury has the obligation to repurchase it on December 31 two years later. The Treasury

147

can obtain the cash to make the repurchase by selling another $1,000 T-note (or T-bill, which has a maturity of twelve months or less, or a T-bond that matures over twenty to thirty years) Businesses do the same thing, replacing matured debt with new debt.

Reducing the public debt of a country with its own currency is a policy choice, not a policy necessity. To understand why reducing public debt rarely occurs we must first complete clarifying "debt burden." If governments need not repay public debt, then the direct cost of the debt equals the interest charges, which governments pay out of current taxes. Assessing whether the interest cost involves a burden on taxpaying citizens takes us to the dual character of debt, as an asset and a liability.

To continue with a US example, consider the case in which income from all sources and ownership of the public debt were equally distributed across households. The Internal Revenue Service would collect taxes from each household and pass the revenue to the Treasury, which would use part of it to pay the interest on outstanding public debt. The net effect would be as if there were no debt – what the IRS took in tax it would return as interest payments. But income distribution across US households is extremely unequal. As long as all interest goes to US households, the public debt involves no burden for society, though its distributive effect is inequitable.

The tax extracted from citizens and businesses to pay the interest on public debt goes back to citizens and businesses as the return on the public securities they hold. The problematical effect lies in the distributional effect. The average US bond holder has an income above that of the average taxpayer. Most people would judge this regressive distributional effect of public interest

## Taxes Are a Burden

Total = $20.2 trillion/106% of GDP

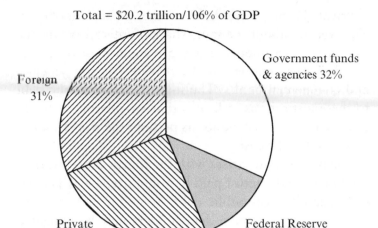

*Figure 5.4 Distribution of the US federal government debt, 2017*

Source: US Treasury Department.

payments as undesirable. The effective solution to the problem is progressive taxation, not lower debt.

Figure 5.4 makes the hypothetical example concrete. Of the total US public debt in 2017 of $20.2 trillion, agencies and special funds of the federal government held 32 percent. The single largest of these was the Social Security Trust Fund, the national retirement program (14 percent). The Federal Reserve System, the US central bank, held an additional 12 percent. As one would expect, the distribution of interest payments closely matches the distribution of debt. It follows that two-fifths of US government interest payments involve a mere recycling of funds. The interest paid to federal agencies such as the Federal Reserve System returns to the Treasury as revenue.

Private US businesses hold another 25 percent of debt. They receive about the same share of interest payments. The three most important US private interest recipients in 2017 were mutual funds, private pension schemes and commercial banks. The importance of public debt to these institutions indicates that speculators in financial markets treat US bonds as perhaps the world's safest way to hold idle cash.

The burden issue arises with the fourth category, debt holding by and interest paid to non-citizens – 31 percent of outstanding US public debt. Some but not many of these nominally foreign debt holders may be obligated to pay US tax on the interest they receive. As a result, interest payments to foreign debt holders represent an unrequited financial outflow from the United States. In 2017 the US Treasury paid interest equal to 3 percent of GDP. This implies a transfer of tax revenue of 0.9 percent of GDP to foreigners (3 percent times 0.31).

This figure, 0.9 percent of GDP, represents the concrete direct cost of the US public debt. In the United Kingdom, the government held 23 percent of its own debt, while foreign debt owners held 27 percent (figure 5.5). In this case the interest outflow is lower than that for the United States – 0.6 percent of GDP. In both cases the foreign ownership share increased substantially over twenty years. In 2000, foreign ownership of US debt was 18 percent compared to the 2018 share of 31 percent; for the UK it was 20 percent, well under the 27 percent in 2017.

These changes indicate that the ownership of UK and US debt by foreigners, and therefore the interest outflow, reflects a policy subject to adjustment. A government could by law restrict bond purchases to buyers liable to

# Taxes Are a Burden

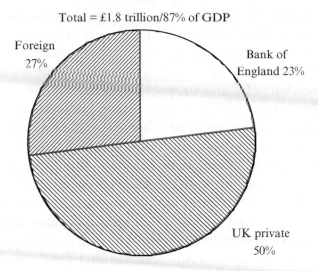

Total = £1.8 trillion/87% of GDP

Foreign 27%

Bank of England 23%

UK private 50%

*Figure 5.5  Distribution of the UK government gross debt, 2017*

Source: Bank of England.

national tax or require all buyers to pay tax wherever they reside. If interest outflow involves a burden on taxpayers, policies can reduce or even eliminate that burden.

While national policy can reverse the shift towards a rising share of debt held by foreigners, that trend reflects a structural trend in global trade. In the twenty-first century, several major countries generated substantial and persistent trade surpluses. Towards the end of the 2010s three countries had annual trade surpluses in excess of $100 billion: China (about 400 billion), Germany (280 billion) and Russia (115 billion). The German government could hold its foreign currency reserves in the relatively stable and fully convertible euro. For the Chinese government, whose currency was not fully convertible, the US dollar and UK pound offered by far the safest liquid assets, with Treasury bills and Bank of England gilts the form in which to hold them Should large trade surpluses continue, we can expect foreign ownership of US and UK public debt to continue.

In contrast to the United States and the United Kingdom, governments of countries without a national currency face a quite different situation, with fewer policy options. Within the European Union the euro-zone countries provide an example worth pursuing analytically. EU treaties prohibit member governments from introducing measures that restrict the flow of the common currency among them. The treaties also specify that member governments cannot fund public spending by borrowing from their national central banks, which means that national bond sales occur in financial markets.

As a result of these treaty limitations, when the global crisis hit Europe in 2008, causing recessions in national economies and contracting public revenue across the continent, national governments had to cover their budget deficits by borrowing from commercial banks. In contrast, the majority of crisis borrowing in the US and the UK came from their central banks (open market operations and quantitative easing; see chapter 1). Because German and French banks dominate European financial markets, the governments of several smaller EU countries found themselves overwhelmingly in debt to banks registered in those countries.

In the mid- and late 2010s, at least 90 percent of Greek government interest payments involved finan-cial outflow, averaging about 3 percent of GDP. For the Portuguese government the figure crept close to 4 percent in some years. Even for the relatively large economy of Italy unrequited outflows approached 3 percent. These are clear cases in which the concept of a debt burden takes on relevance. In the United Kingdom, the United States and other countries with national currencies, it has almost no relevance.

## From Myth to Reality

The "taxes are a burden" narrative derives from a basic fallacy, that governments extract tax from citizens by compulsion, while people voluntarily spend out of their income. This fallacy presumes what it seeks to prove, that people make their private expenditures voluntarily but have no control over public expenditures. In many cases the reverse is true.

In a dissent to a 1927 US Supreme Court case, the famous jurist Oliver Wendell Holmes wrote: "Taxes are the price we pay for civilization." The quotation indicates that this chapter began with the wrong premise. Instead of initiating the discussion from the perspective of the individual, an appropriate beginning would have been a societal vision.

At all levels, and for all functions, people find themselves enmeshed in a division of labor. The economic division of labor receives the greatest attention. In a campaign speech in July 2012, US President Barack Obama told an audience in Roanoke, Virginia: "If you've got a business – you didn't build that." While not up to his usually eloquent standard, this statement, aggressively attacked by Republican politicians and right-wingers in general, conveyed an important truth.

# Taxes Are a Burden

Earlier, in a 2011 speech in Andover, Massachusetts, Elizabeth Warren, later US Senator from that state, stated the same truth with greater force and clarity:

> There is nobody in this country who got rich on his own – nobody. You built a factory out there? Good for you. But I want to be clear. You moved your goods to market on the roads the rest of us paid for. You hired workers the rest of us paid to educate. You were safe in your factory because of police-forces and fire-forces that the rest of us paid for. You didn't have to worry that marauding bands would come and seize everything at your factory – and hire someone to protect against this – because of the work the rest of us did. Now look, you built a factory and it turned into something terrific, or a great idea. God bless – keep a big hunk of it. But part of the underlying social contract is, you take a hunk of that and pay forward for the next kid who comes along.

On one level this message comes across as disarmingly simple: what each person achieves requires the contribution of others. The simple message contains a far more profound one, which I developed in chapter 3. Each person is born, lives and dies within a set of social relations and social responsibilities from which we cannot be extracted. The fallacy of the "taxes are a burden" myth has its basis in treating people as what they are not, individuals extracted out of the society that created and maintains them.

Societies consist of citizens who, acting through democratic institutions, can solve collective problems such as unemployment, poverty and inequality. Central to that belief is the nature of the economy – it is not the sum of individual actions. Quite to the contrary, individual actions in part result from the constraints

# Taxes Are a Burden

set by social values and the state of the economy itself.

Viewing people primarily as consumers who loathe tax rather than as citizens of a democratic society denies the importance of individual–societal interaction. It is the source of the "taxes are a burden" fallacy. If people were first and foremost consumers, then taxation would fall as a burden on them because it reduces their buying power. "People are consumers" reflects two fallacies: 1) that tax funds expenditure; and 2) that private provision is always more appropriate than public provision.

The vast majority of private expenditure by the vast majority of citizens goes to the necessities of life. These involve voluntary choices in the limited but important sense that households have some flexibility to satisfy those necessities. Households also have choices as to whether to fund important services by market purchases or through taxation. A decision by a majority of citizens not to fund university education publicly, for example, and reduce taxes equivalently does not reduce the burden on household finances. The direct financial effect is to shift the burden from the taxes households pay to household private expenditure.

For those who ideologically prefer private provision, that majority decision may seem a benefit, but the benefit does not come in lower expenditure. On the contrary, for many essential services – education, health and transport – the public provision option frequently involves a lower tax payment than the superficially equivalent private payment. The private payment is "superficially" equivalent because, as argued above, the public and private sectors rarely provide the same service even when it has the same description.

155

# Taxes Are a Burden

At the beginning of this chapter I offered a quotation from the US Tax Foundation that sought to define the year in terms of its anti-government ideology, dividing the employed person's time by taxation. Once we recognize that what is not funded through tax must be covered by the household through private purchases, I can restate that time line, based on the distribution of UK public expenditure in table 5.1.

> The average UK employee spends the first eighty-nine days along with other citizens funding public health care, education, insurance against unemployment, pension for old age and security of the community, then 117 private days to transport, feed, house, heat and clothe the family, before enjoying the twenty-eight days of paid holiday guaranteed by government regulation.

By analogous calculation, the US average worker spends only sixty-eight days in the funding of collective services ("working to pay tax"), leaving 182 days of work to cover private expenditures ("freedom days"), followed by a meager ten days of public holiday. Worth adding in this vein is that the average British employee worked the notional equivalent of seventeen days to fund health care, almost all of it through the public sector (the National Health Service). The equivalent calculation for the American employee was double, thirty-five days.

Shifting provision from public to private funding involves no reduction of the burden on citizens. It reflects a political choice of how people and the community reproduce and fulfill themselves. Maintaining an orderly society based on humane principles does not come without cost. Social expenditure equitably distributed provides the foundation for that society. That expenditure keeps at bay what Thomas Hobbes, in *Leviathan* (1651), described as society in the absence of a social contract, when human life was "solitary, poor, nasty, brutish and short." Or, to repeat Justice Holmes, "Taxes are the price we pay for civilization." The "burden" we carry is not taxation but civilization.

# 6

# Austerity: There is No Alternative

## *The Myth Itself*

The best economic management may be for national governments to set expenditure and tax, not to balance budgets, but to keep the economy close to its full capacity with low unemployment. But, get real. This is not the time for the "best" policy; it is the time to prevent disaster. The global financial crisis of 2008–10 created circumstances which changed the game forever. With a large public debt hanging over us, and growing larger due to unmanageable deficits, the economy faced and faces dire threats, collapse of the currency, inflation, unserviceable debt and loss of market confidence. Until we bring public finances under control we remain on the cliff-edge of government bankruptcy.

These are not joking matters, bordering on and including the worst disasters that could strike a society short of war. While not jokes, they are figments of over-heated rhetoric generated by ignorance of how modern economies function. We now have the analytical tools

158

to put these imagined maladies back into their box. All these disasters have inflicted harm on countries from time to time. Understanding the conditions when they occur allows us to recognize their infrequency. Driving an automobile is dangerous. But with knowledge and caution accidents rarely occur. The same applies to economic management of potential instability in modern economies.

The comparison of household budgets with government budgets finds its fullest expression in anxieties about public debt and the possible, indeed likely, negative effects on that debt on our economy, society and families. These anxieties refer to circumstances extremely unlikely in countries whose monetary systems are based on national currencies managed by a national central bank. The anxieties arise from myth, not reality.

## Public Debt Disasters

As repeatedly explained in this book, a government with its public debt in its own currency will never fall into default. When a government borrows in a foreign currency it makes itself vulnerable to default. The reason is quite straightforward, illustrated by a concrete example.

In 2011, after receiving debt reduction as part of an international initiative applied to many low-income countries, the public debt of the Republic of Zambia fell to below 20 percent of GDP. In the context of rising copper prices, the overwhelming source of the country's export earnings, Zambian governments sold bonds in European financial markets denominated in euros, which drove the debt share to near 60 percent of GDP.

International copper prices behave in a strongly cyclical manner. When high, Zambian foreign exchange earnings flowed in robustly. However, when the copper price began to decline, the Zambian government faced increasing difficulty in servicing its euro-denominated debt.

That simple story, borrowing in a foreign currency and then suffering from a fall in export revenue, explains the overwhelming majority of international defaults on national public debt. To this majority we can add a few pathological cases, such as that of Zimbabwe at the end of the 1990s and into the 2000s. The combination of hyperinflation and bankruptcy resulted from the country's irresolvable political conflict. When citizens and businesses revolt by refusing to pay their taxes and the government lacks the legitimacy to force collection, what follows is economic and social disaster. Debt default as a result of civil strife and war has little relevance to the vast majority of countries, least of all to North America and Europe (though perhaps one should not be too complacent).

Over the last half-century, a few governments have found themselves with unsustainable debt. The people in their countries have suffered severely as a result of the measures taken to resolve the dilemma. "Dilemma" is the appropriate word – a choice between two alternatives which prove undesirable. All cases of unsustainable public debt have a common feature. The government contracted part or all of the public debt in a currency it did not control. This common feature has two variations: a government that does not have a currency it controls and one that has a currency it controls but chooses to borrow in some other currency.

160

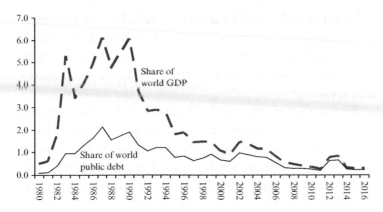

*Figure 6.1  Value of debt defaults, 1980–2016 (percentage of world public bonds and world GDP)*

Source· Bank of Canada, *Technical Report 101,* 2017.

Before embarking on our analysis, it should be stressed that, while governments do on occasion default on their debts, it occurs rarely with limited impact beyond the country defaulting. In 2017, the Bank of Canada, the country's central bank, published a study cataloguing government defaults. Figure 6.1 reports the relevant statistics. In the 1980s many governments partially defaulted on their debts. This cluster of defaults occurred as part of the Latin American debt crisis, though there were defaulters from other regions, for example the Republic of Korea in East Asia. Two trends in the 1970s laid the basis for defaults in the next decade. First, rapidly rising primary product prices led to a substantial accumulation of dollars for many developing-country governments. This accumulation gave the impression that those governments enjoyed strong economies, capable of servicing external debt. Second, oil was one of the primary products whose price rose

161

substantially, leading to dollar accumulations by petroleum exporters far in excess of what they could spend.
These "petro dollars" flowed into banks in Western
Europe and North America (in both the United States
and Canada).

To pay the interest on the deposits of the governments
of oil-producing countries, banks sought borrowers who
would pay them interest. In those bygone days, financial
regulation, especially in the United States, severely limited to whom banks could lend. Regulations did not
restrict lending to foreign governments, which made the
governments enjoying price booms in non-oil primary
exports apparently ideal clients. Unfortunately for both
borrower and lender, at the beginning of the 1980s the
primary product boom came to an abrupt end. Policy-
induced recessions in the United States and the United
Kingdom played a substantial role in the end of "commodity boom" era, recessions designed to reverse the
inflation generated largely by oil prices.

Figure 6.1 shows the result, the value of defaulted debt
rising to well over 5 percent of world GDP in the 1980s,
then tailing off through the 1990s. By the new century
defaults had dropped to insubstantial levels. Important
for our understanding of the possible danger of default
is that, during the thirty-six years, only three devel-
oped-country governments were among the defaulters,
Greece (2012, 2013, 2015), Ireland (2013) and Portugal
(2013). All three countries used the euro at the time of
their defaults, which has a simple explanation that we
elaborate in the next section.

Before wading into the causes of debt default, the
term itself needs clarification. Debt default occurs when
a government fails to service its debt as contractu-

ally required. For example, if a government misses a contractually required payment or pays only part of the scheduled debt service, it has defaulted. A default can result from conscious policy, from unanticipated circumstances, or through formal agreement with the creditor. Defaults by formal agreement involve various forms of rescheduling and restructuring. For example, an agreement can result in repayments stretching out over a longer time period or replacing the original debt with bonds carrying more flexible repayment conditions.

### *Euro Debt Crisis and the TINA Principle*

Given that only eurozone members among developed countries have fallen into default in recent years, the discussion of debt disasters begins with them. First floated as a possibility as far back as the 1960s, the euro began its formal existence as a unit of account in 1999. It is doubtful that the original members of the eurozone foresaw the full implications of what they had joined.

Now an oft-told tale, in the early 2010s several governments of eurozone countries found themselves with unmanageable budget deficits and unmanageable public debt. Confronted with those problems, the European Commission, the executive wing of the European Union, informed those governments that they had to reduce their budget deficits immediately and pay down their debts. Converting budget deficits into surpluses would generate the euros to buy back the excessive debts bit by bit. The process carried heavy social and economic costs, lower public funding for health and education, economic slowdown and contraction, and unemployment.

The deficits had to end and debt be reduced. As painful as the corrective medicine might prove, "there is/was no alternative," the TINA principle. Pursuing the euro zone deficit and debt crisis provides considerable insight into the operation and application of that principle.

I begin with figure 6.2, which indicates the potential dangers in surrendering control over one's currency. It traces the interest rates on the bonds of seven eurozone countries and the United Kingdom. To keep the graphic simple, figure 6.2 reports the average rates for Greece, Ireland, Italy, Portugal and Spain, as well as the average for France and Germany, with the UK rate on its own. Several key characteristics of the European Union and, within it, the eurozone that frequently go unstated are revealed.

To make sense of why the bond rates of five euro countries went through the roof while those for two others continued low and stable, we need to remind ourselves of the rules of operation of the European common currency and the European Central Bank which seeks to manage it. As we shall see, the central message coming out of figure 6.2 is one of political, not economic causality.

The euro began with ten member countries and reached nineteen in 2015, when the Lithuanian government joined. Germany ranks as by far the largest member, with a population of 82 million and a GDP of €3.8 trillion. The smallest member, Malta, would qualify as a medium-sized German town (population 429,000 and GDP €8.9 billion). While the nineteen countries use the same currency, responsibility for public bonds falls on each government. There is no "euro bond" in the singular. The European Central Bank, like all central banks, takes exclusive responsibility for the common currency. Unlike national central banks, it is not allowed to purchase public bonds. Each government takes responsibility for the bonds it issues.

This combination of common currency and national bonds carries important implications. EU treaties prohibit national central banks from purchasing their government's bonds. Were they allowed to do so, it would imply that national central banks could create euros in the same way that governments of countries with national currencies can. Thus, the limitation on a government operating within a currency union such as the euro comes from political limitations, not the technical characteristics of national versus common currencies.

The restrictions on national central banks lending to their governments has a clear purpose. Were this allowed without restriction, the central monetary authority would surrender its control over the currency. The actions of a central bank in a small country – Malta would be the obvious example – would have little impact across the eurozone, but those in a large country – Spain for example – would have substantial spread effects, provoking inflation and depreciating the euro. However, a complete ban on "monetizing" public spending at the national level may be too restrictive.

As practically reasonable as the monopoly control by the European Central Bank (ECB) on creating euros may be, it results in a "one size fits all" monetary policy. The eurozone consists of countries of markedly different size and great variation in levels of development. As

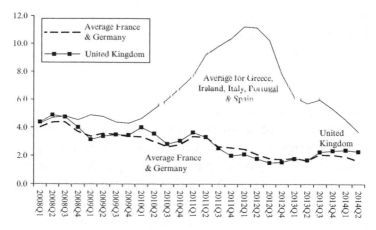

*Figure 6.2 Interest rates on long-term public bonds, seven eurozone countries and the UK, 2008(Q1)–2014(Q2)*

*Source:* Eurostat.

a result, national governments are left to adjust as best they can to ECB monetary policy. Twenty years of the operation of the euro suggests that the more developed large countries adjust more easily than the others.

With these points in mind we can inspect figure 6.2. As the global economic storm gathered force in 2008, the public debt levels among the seven eurozone countries shown were quite different. The EU treaty-specified measure of public debt for Greece and Italy stood at over 100 percent of GDP (119 and 115 percent, respectively), while Ireland and Spain both remained just below 50 percent, considerably lower than for Germany (68 percent). At 83 percent, the Portuguese debt lay in the middle among those five, about the same as for France (81 percent).

During the first half of 2008, as the global recession unfolded, interest rates on the bonds of all eight countries in figure 6.2 were about the same, with the UK rate the lowest. At the end of that year divergence began and through 2009 showed a relatively modest difference. In 2010 the speculative meltdown began, first for Greece. A 5 percent rate on Greek government bonds at the end of 2009 rose to 11 percent a year later, and in mid-2012 hit its peak, at 25 percent. As the bond rate soared, the Bank of Greece could do nothing to stop it.

Over the next two years the speculative attacks on public bonds spread, in a manner that demonstrated clearly the vulnerability of small countries compared to large ones. Irish public bonds next suffered speculative assault. From 5 percent in mid-2010, the Irish bond rate ballooned to over 10 percent a year later. By contrast, in Spain, with almost the same pre-crisis public debt, the speculation-driven rise in bond rates came later and passed quickly, briefly rising above 6 percent in mid-2012, then dropping back below 5 percent and below 3 percent in 2014.

The experience of Italy and Portugal was even more superficially anomalous. Entering 2010 with public debt 100 percent of GDP, Portuguese bonds quickly came under pressure, reaching 6.6 percent at the end of that year, then 12 percent at the end of 2011. Meanwhile, Italian bonds, "burdened" by a 130 percent debt to GDP ratio in 2009, prompted no speculative assault for two years and then quite mild when it occurred. The Italian bond rate hit its peak at 6.6 percent in the last quarter of 2011, when the less indebted Portuguese government would pay 12 percent (and still rising), and the much less indebted Irish government faced 8.4 percent.

EU treaties blocked all possible lines of defense for the five governments suffering speculative attacks on their bonds. The basic problem was not the size of public debt, which varied substantially across countries. Whether debts were high (as in Greece and Italy) or low (Ireland and Spain), the power of financial speculation was a problem facing all the governments. Removing public bonds from the power of financial markets was the obvious solution to the problem. Had the EU treaty rules been more flexible, national governments would have had several alternative policies to implement.

If the treaties allowed national governments the option of selling bonds to their central banks, that in a stroke could have ended upward pressure on interest rates. As the eponymous financial markets drove up bond rates, the Bank of Italy, for example, could have intervened and offered to purchase bonds at a fixed rate, such as that prevailing before the financial crisis hit in 2008.

There are two objections to that policy alternative. First, allowing national central banks to create euros might undermine the authority of the European Central Bank, permanently damaging its ability to implement a common monetary policy. As clumsy as the ECB's "one size fits all" monetary policy might be, the need for a common currency to have a central authority is a persuasive argument. If we accept that argument, there remains an alternative to exposing public bonds to financial speculation. The ECB could allow national central banks to buy their government's bonds only if the purchase did not increase euros in circulation.

That requirement would seem impossible – by definition bond purchases create new money. The impossible becomes possible through a monetary trick. The term "sterilization" in monetary policy refers to central bank action that prevents open market operations (see chapter 1) from impacting on the supply of money. When a central bank purchases a bond from a non-government holder, that purchase exchanges cash for "government paper." The central bank can cancel – "sterilize" – that increase by matching the bond purchase with a sale (in which the central bank exchanges a new bond for money from the private sector).

To a sensible person, sterilization may appear little more than sleight of hand – why should a central bank purchase a bond from the private sector, then immediately turn around and sell one? This simple question has a simple answer: the central bank has a different purpose when it buys a bond than it does when it sells. The purchase would have the purpose of preventing the bond rate from rising. The central bank makes the purchase to prevent a private-sector sale that drives up the bond rate. The subsequent bond purchase aims to eliminate the cash in circulation created by the sale.

What if the national central bank tries this trick, purchase and sale, but it doesn't work? For example, the national central bank successfully prevents a rise in the national bond rate by serving as buyer of "first resort." However, when it seeks to sterilize the cash it has put into circulation, private buyers refuse to purchase the new bond at the prevailing rate.

If the first two alternatives fail, a third remains. The European Central Bank could have intervened to purchase national bonds at a fixed rate, immediately ending financial speculation in every country, just as the Bank of England and the US Federal Reserve System have done in their countries from time to time. This action would have ended the eurozone crisis immediately, requiring no other intervention.

169

Austerity: There is No Alternative

In 2011 the government of Greece faced a problem: speculative attack on its bonds that drove interest rates to an unmanageable level. Doing nothing was not an option. In Brussels and Berlin, EU leaders diagnosed the problem as one of excessive public debt that required severe budgetary austerity to turn deficit into surplus in order to pay down the debt. The designers of the austerity argued that "there is no alternative" (TINA). When the Greek government began to implement the EU's TINA policy, the country's debt was 160 percent of national income (GDP). At the end of 2017, after six years of TINA austerity, the Greek debt has risen to 176 percent of GDP. Even more unsettling, as the Greek government sought to implement austerity policies, one by one four other governments faced the same speculative assaults.

The austerity policy failed in five countries to solve the problem it set for itself. There were alternatives. Those who controlled policy rejected the alternatives. The debt crisis among eurozone countries resulted not from debt itself. It resulted from conscious political decisions to pursue a failing policy. When policy derives from pragmatic problem solving rather than from abstract imperatives such as the TINA principle, governments avoid defaults.

### Fear of Deficits and Inflation

Because the United States, the United Kingdom and other countries such as Japan have national currencies, they can prevent speculative attacks on their bonds and, therefore, defaults. However, that doesn't change the fact

170

that deficits create inflationary dangers. Deficits mean spending money that the government does not have. And that means printing money, which is inflationary.

It is not a fact that deficits provoke inflation; nor is it correct that deficit spending involves creating – "printing" – money. More important than these two factual mistakes, the commonly invoked link between deficit and inflation reflects a deep misunderstanding by politicians, the media and the public. Perhaps no common economic phenomenon is so misunderstood and misrepresented than inflation. Were the proverbial person in the street asked for an explanation of inflation, the likely response would be "too much money chasing too few goods."

That clichéd phrase implies what might be called the "Bathtub Theory of Inflation." Imagine a bathtub with tick marks on the inside to measure how full it is. Let the tub half fill with water with a large number of plastic ducks floating in it, each with a label such as "breakfast cereal," "milk," "automobile tires," and so on. The water represents money in this analogy and the tick marks measure the price level. Turning on a tap raises prices and lifting the plug to let water out brings prices down.

As far-fetched as the bathtub analogy may appear, it represents a simplified form of the prevailing approach to inflation – the quantity theory of money, sometimes also called the quantity equation of exchange. The bathtub analogy neatly encapsulates the analysis of inflation that has held much of the economics profession in its grip for generations. Note that, as the water level rises or falls, all the plastic ducks rise and fall by the same amount. "Neutrality" is the somewhat esoteric term for this in the theory of money – an increase in the money supply raises all prices the same.

From this simple, easily grasped analysis, linking inflation to deficits follows naturally. Deficits increase the amount of money in circulation, which leaves more money chasing the same amount of goods and services. That hot pursuit may prompt greater output for some goods and services, but, if production is inflexible, the result is inflation. As reasonable as this simple sequence may seem, and as much weight is assigned to it by professional economists, it is an abstraction that bears little relation to the real world of price movements.

We start again with a real-world approach to prices and inflation. The goods and services that people buy fall into two broad categories. Those strongly influenced by international markets are called by economists "tradables," which refers to their characteristic of moving in international trade. I will use the more straightforward adjective "international." The other category is "domestic" goods and services ("non-tradables"), whose prices are little affected by international markets.

Petroleum jumps out as the most important international item, its price in each country being determined almost entirely by international markets. In open economies such as the United States, the United Kingdom and the members of the European Union, international exchange to some degree influences almost every good, be it agricultural or manufactured. Services provide most of the items in the domestic category – for transport, housing and education. A municipal government can import a bus for public transport but not the cross-town bus ride on 42nd Street in Manhattan. Similarly, a builder can import the materials to construct a block of

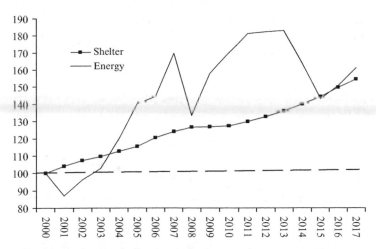

*Figure 6.3 Two components of the US consumer price index, 2000–2017*

Source: Economic Report of the President 2018.

flats in London, but the housing service itself is purely domestic, with its rent influenced only marginally by cross-border transactions. A very wealthy rentier may mull over the rents and property prices in London and Paris, but for the overwhelming majority relocating is not a serious option.

Figure 6.3 shows the movement of two categories in the US consumer price index, the domestic service "shelter" and the international composite good "energy." Both begin in 2000 at an index of 100, and seventeen years later their increases closely match, at 55 percent and 61 percent respectively. However, between 2000 and 2017, energy shows quite volatile fluctuations, while the growth of shelter cost continues at a slow and steady pace. If we ignore the negative signs (in mathematics jargon, use "absolute values"), over the eighteen

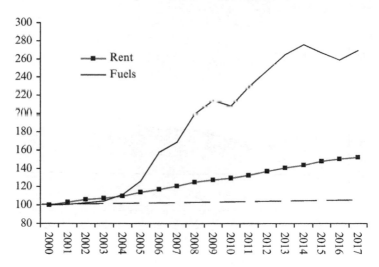

*Figure 6.4 Two components of the UK consumer price index, 2000–2017*

Source: Office for National Statistics.

years the annual average price of shelter increased at 2.6 percent, while the energy variation averaged over 10 percent (10.2 to be exact). For example, in 2008 energy prices fell by 24 percent, then rose the following year by 17 percent. For shelter in the same years the price changes were 0.2 and 2.5 percent.

Figure 6.4 presents similar categories for the United Kingdom and shows a more extreme difference between the domestic and the international. Over the eighteen years 2000–17, the index for the domestic "rental" category rose at 2.3 percent per year, far below the 6.2 percent rate for "fuels." For both countries the two categories capture the domestic–international distinction but are not the same for what is included. The US "shelter" category includes home prices and mortgage costs, while the UK measure excludes these. The composition of the "energy" and "fuels" also has substantial differences. US subsidies for hydrocarbon extraction also complicate the "energy" and "fuel" comparison.

These differences do not undermine the central point – the behavior of international prices can vary substantially from the behavior of domestic prices. When we recognize this difference in behavior, the concept of inflation becomes considerably more complex. What the media cite as inflation derives from an averaging of price changes across all goods and services. The statisticians obtain this average using "weights" derived from household surveys. These weights themselves are averages, which has an extremely important implication. A few national statistics offices calculate household expenditure weights for different levels of income.

This is not the practice in the United States, the United Kingdom or the European Union. Statistics from the US demonstrate the potential bias in using average weights. A Congressional Budget Office study, *The Distribution of Household Income*, estimated average household income in 2014 at $91,500. But a household reached that income level at the sixty-eighth percentile of the distribution – two-thirds of households had incomes lower than the income level used for estimating expenditure weights. For the UK, the calculation of the equivalent distribution point for expenditure weights also fell close to two-thirds of the way up the household distribution. The implication should be obvious. The inflation measure used in most advanced countries refers to the expenditures of the upper middle class, not the typical (median) household, and even less those on low incomes.

A 2 percent increase in the rate of officially measured inflation is not what it seems for at least three reasons. First, that number reflects the spending behavior of households well up the income distribution. Second, the increase may reflect price changes in only a few goods which carry heavy weight in the price index and have volatile fluctuations due to instability in international markets. In 2009 in the United States, food prices excluding meals in restaurants fell by 2.4 percent and shelter costs increased by a meager 0.3 percent. These two categories account for a large proportion of spending by lower income groups. Yet the overall consumer price index rose by 2.7 percent (from the *Economic Report of the President 2018*, Table 10). The previous year showed the reverse anomaly. In 2008 the overall CPI barely rose (0.1 percent), even though shelter costs increased by 1.9 percent and food by 6.6 percent.

The third reason derives from the second. In 2008–9 the US central bank, the Federal Reserve, had an inflation target of 2 percent. Had the "Fed" applied that target in 2009 strictly, it would have implied policies to suppress inflation as officially measured, which it did not, recognizing that a sudden 20 percent increase in energy prices accounted almost entirely for the above-target rate. Drawing on the distinction between international and domestic prices, a general lesson emerges from the US price movements during those two years. Official price measures on which central banks base their inflation targets include prices over which those central banks have almost no control.

What happens when a central bank – the Fed, the Bank of England or the European Central Bank – seeks to drive down an inflation rate whose increase results from prices over which those banks have little or no control? The impact of its inflation-suppressing action falls on those prices over which it does have control – domestic services. Wages represent the largest cost component of domestic services. It follows that a central bank attempt to suppress internationally driven inflation is in practice a wage-suppression policy. An example makes this generalization concrete. During the eight years before the global crash, 2000–7, the US consumer price index exceeded the 2 percent target in six years. In every case but one the official inflation rate breached the 2 percent level because of increases in energy prices in excess of 10 percent (as before, statistics form the *Economic Report of the President 2018*).

Our dissection of inflation and how governments measure it produces an important conclusion. Except when civil strife hits and public order breaks down, above-target inflation does not result from excessive public spending. It results from the international transmission of commodity prices, almost always energy prices.

Two nails remain to seal the coffin of inflation anxieties in advanced countries. First, a 2 percent measured increase in prices using official methodology is not 2 percent inflation. The first nail will occur to anyone who has an automobile. Prices for new automobiles at the end of the 2010s were considerably higher than they were at the turn of the century. The price increases resulted from changes in the quality of the automobile, especially the computerizing of many functions. In 2018 the car buyer purchased a different product than would have been purchased in 2000 (a fact demonstrated daily to me when I drive my 2000 model Nissan Micra).

In the 1990s, the US Congress commissioned a study of the possible bias in the consumer price index through not accounting for quality change. A study in 1996, the Boskin Report, concluded that the consumer price index overstated inflation by 1.1 percent during the 1990s (a measured rate of inflation of 2 percent falls to 0.9 percent when adjusted for changes in the quality of goods and services). But the Boskin Report led to no substantial changes in how US government statisticians measured inflation. In no advanced country does the official inflation rate adjust for quality changes.

Because of the rapid transfer of production techniques and products among advanced countries, we can conservatively estimate that the almost ubiquitous 2 percent inflation target of central banks represents an effective rate of half that. Of even more importance to the credibility of a 2 percent target is the second nail for the inflation-suppression coffin. In the feudal system, the institutionally constrained markets for land and labor severely limited shifting productive resources. In the erstwhile centrally planned economies, bureaucrats dictated allocation. The dynamism of market economies lies in their flexibility to reallocate resources as conditions change.

Markets reallocate resources through price changes. As new products appear, some companies decline and others expand, and the expanding companies attract workers from those in decline by offering higher pay. Because nominal wages more easily rise than fall, an "inflation" in pay is the empirical result of labor reallocation. To suppress the overall inflationary impact of this reallocation process inherent in market economies means suppressing the system's growth dynamic.

## Austerity: There is No Alternative

It is quite possible that, among its other malign effects, inflation targeting by central banks in North America and Europe can justifiably claim credit for the sluggish recovery and low growth in productivity after the global crisis.

"Deficits are inflationary, inflation hurts everyone, so there is no alternative to austerity." After repeated myth-busting, this statement cannot stand. Deficits are not inflationary. Inflation does not hurt everyone, and there are many alternatives to austerity. One more deficit- and inflation-linked anxiety requires inspection: the commonly expressed view that deficits cause deterioration in the "strength" of a country's currency. I place "strength" in quotation marks because this anxiety over deficit effects begins with an invalid premise, that a "strong" exchange rate – for example lots of Canadian dollars to the US dollar – is desirable.

In autumn 2016, after British voters rejected membership of the European Union, the pound fell sharply against other major currencies. A prominent British economist, a former member of the Monetary Policy Committee of the Bank of England, expressed the "strong currency" mantra in notably simple form: "the pound is the share price of UK plc" (found in an article in *The Guardian*, 14 October 2016; plc is the British equivalent of "incorporated"). While this is a rather strange turn of phrase – few citizens anywhere view their countries as corporations – it does encapsulate the belief that strengthening of the national currency is good and weakening it is bad.

A brief consideration of what determines currency rates across countries helps to dispel the strong dollar, pound, etc., fallacy. During the years 1945 to 1970,

179

most advanced countries maintained some form of control over financial flows, which severely limited their size. In addition, almost all governments were members of the International Monetary Fund, which required fixed exchange rates linked to the US dollar. Exchange rates typically changed as a result of an unsustainable trade deficit. The devaluation of the British pound in 1967 from $2.80 to $2.40 sought to correct an unsustainable balance of international payments.

However, with the elimination of controls in the 1970s and the 1980s, the importance of trade in the determination of exchange rates declined, to be replaced by a massive rise in financial flows. A substantial portion of financial flows move in and out of countries with rapid turnover. In the short-run these large financial movements, speculation, can have a substantial impact on exchange rates. The destabilizing effect of financial flows provides the basis for arguments, such as the "share price" analogy, that business confidence (sometimes "investor" confidence) is an important determination of exchange rates.

If to this speculation phenomenon we add the presumption that government deficits undermine business confidence, then it follows that deficits undermine the strength of a currency. This view suffers from several shortcomings. First, it presumes that exchange rates reflect the subjective judgments of speculators rather than the operation of the national economy in its entirety. While much more complex in their determination, exchange rates, as for other simpler prices such as those in supermarkets, embody a core set of factors that establish their norm and short-term influences that generate fluctuations about that norm.

Austerity: There is No Alternative

In this framework, would public deficits be the basic determinant of exchange rates or a source of temporary fluctuations? The answer depends on specifying the mechanism by which deficits transmit to the exchange rate. The simplest mechanism offered by some is a variation on "supply and demand." Deficits increase the domestic money supply. An increase in domestic money relative to foreign money drives down the price of the former. This is not a compelling argument because funding deficits by bond sales to the private sector leaves the supply of domestic money unchanged (look back at chapter 1, "How Governments Borrow," p. 29).

What if the government funds expenditure, an increased deficit, by selling the bonds to itself? The domestic money supply will increase by that borrowing. However, more is going on than changes in the money supply and the possible response of the exchange rate. The purpose of the increased expenditure is to stimulate the economy. As the economy grows, the demand for money by the private sector also grows. A vigorous expansion of the economy could result in money demand increasing more than money supply. We have a complex relationship that cannot and should not be reduced to a simplistic one-on-one causality.

If governments pursue foolish policies, the result could be a depreciation ("weakening") of the currency relative to other currencies. Funding a deficit by direct credit from the central bank provides a good example of foolish policy. But responsible management of the public budget as proposed throughout this book leads to sound policies with predictable outcomes. Should outcomes not conform to prediction, corrective measures exist. Public deficits are not ticking time bombs.

181

In many cases they prove more responsible policy outcomes than budget surpluses, and circumstances, not ideology, should determine when each is appropriate.

## *From Myth to Reality*

In his first inaugural address, on 3 March 1933, Franklin D. Roosevelt told Americans: "The only thing we have to fear is fear itself – nameless, unreasoning, unjustified terror which paralyzes needed efforts to convert retreat into advance." The same applies to the fears that drive the TINA principle's justification of austerity.

We have the alternatives to austerity. National governments should set spending and taxation targets to avoid the extremes of recession and inflation. By keeping within the Goldilocks Zone, lodged safely between recession and inflation, democratically elected governments can implement the political and social goals set by their citizens. The economic management principle might be briefly summarized as "balance policies, not budgets." The first step in this approach involves the government specifying its spending plans. Then the government sets tax targets to arrive at and stay in the Goldilocks Zone.

This policy sequence reverses austerity budgeting, which attempts to trim public expenditure to match public revenue. That, the austerity doctrine, takes a country into the inflation zone or leaves resources unnecessarily idle (usually the latter), which comes as an unplanned and perhaps unanticipated outcome. Anti-austerity turns austerity sequencing upside down – first, political debate in a democratic society determines spending priorities, what activities government should deliver to its citizens, the time scale of delivery, and the level of provision. These priorities dictate the expenditure necessary to fulfill them. With spending levels set, the next step involves identifying the level of tax revenue to keep the economy within the Goldilocks Zone, that benign territory between an unacceptable inflation rate and unnecessarily idle resources.

In this approach to spending and taxation, the public budget automatically contributes to the solution of avoiding extremes. When recession threatens, budgets tend towards deficit, softening the decline of the national economy. Inflation produces the mirror image – rising tax revenues that weaken private spending. Progressive taxation provides the important mechanism that facilitates the benign balance between recession and inflation.

# 7

# Always an Alternative

Cinema buffs may recall a 1958 film titled *Me and the Colonel*, with Danny Kaye in the lead as a Polish Jew, Jacobowsky, fleeing the Nazis (by far his best performance). At several pivotal points in the film Jacobowsky quotes his deceased mother's advice: "in life, there are always two possibilities." The advice of Jacobowsky's mother applies to austerity, though it is an underestimate. Many possibilities exist to avoid the bitter consequences of striving for balanced budgets, possibilities that offer hope and improvement.

Policy frameworks, especially economic policy frameworks, derive from politics, not technical economic principles. The "hard choices" politicians invoke arise in the attempt to reconcile political priorities, not from fallacious economic imperatives. The values of society, manifested through the democratic process, guide and limit the social and political goals that a government can pursue. Whether economic circumstances constrain achieving those values proves more often than not to be a policy choice itself.

Once these goals are clarified, expertise has a role

to play. My purpose has been to reveal that generally accepted policy imperatives do not have their basis in expertise. They come from political decisions. Much discussion and elaboration leads to a clear conclusion: balancing the public budget is not a policy imperative. Such decisions are political choices, and alternative policies always exist for citizens to choose among. As a country we do not have to "live within our means," because as citizens we have the power to determine our means.

National governments with their own currencies need not "balance the books." On the contrary, taking that principle as a guide to public budgeting invariably produces dysfunctional results and undermines the welfare of citizens. At times citizens face "hard decisions," but these need never require "tightening our belts." Those hard decisions involve reaching political consensus, or at least majority agreement, over the great social and political decisions confronting society – reducing inequality, eliminating discrimination and protecting the global environment.

In pursuit of making those decisions wisely, public debt provides a tool that allows budgetary flexibility as well as a secure haven for storing household and corporate wealth. Public debt enhances the role of taxation, which through its central role in balancing the economy between recession and excessive inflation links the citizen to society.

All the myths dispelled in this book, especially the TINA principle, draw their credibility from two closely related trends that emerged in the late 1970s, one ideological and the other a policy change based on that ideology. Together they fostered what might be called a

185

"decommissioning of public policy tools." Step by step the public policy instruments required to manage the stability and expansion of complex market economies became constrained and limited by TINA like Ideological imperatives. In some cases the legislation acted to reference these constraints and limits. The overall effect was a delegitimizing and discrediting of the public sector to manage the outcomes generated by private markets.

This decommissioning and discrediting reproduced in more strict form the anti-government ideology that prevailed before the Great Depression of the 1930s. Before the Depression, public policy instruments were so severely constrained that they allowed little scope for effective economic management. At the level of the economy as a whole, governments potentially have three sets of economic tools: those that impact on trade and capital flows among countries, those that operate through the budgetary process, and those that attempt to influence the monetary system. Up to the Great Depression, ideology preached that governments should tie exchange rates for currencies to an international gold mechanism, that public budgets should balance, and that central banks should guard against inflation.

### Decommissioning Exchange Rates

For most of the twentieth century national governments operated international transactions with fixed exchange rates, based either on gold (into the 1930s) or the US dollar. The US dollar link was established towards the end of World War II. In 1944 the governments of countries with market economies formalized fixed exchange rates in what became known as the Bretton Woods System (named after a resort in the US state of New Hampshire). Every government joining the International Monetary Fund, created by the Bretton Woods System, pledged to maintain an exchange rate fixed to the US dollar. As the linchpin in the system, the US government guaranteed a price for gold of $35 per ounce (established in 1933 by the first Roosevelt presidency). In principle and in practice, any member government of the IMF could redeem gold for the dollars it held, though the Gold Reserve Act of 1934 prohibited US residents from owning gold.

At first glance it might appear that a fixed exchange-rate system limited public policy. In practice, fixed rates created an important policy tool for managing the stability of the economy. While governments were committed to maintaining fixed rates to the dollar, they had the flexibility to change the rate. The US government was the sole exception because it managed the currency on which all others were calculated. In most cases governments "devalued," thus increasing the units of the national currency that a dollar would purchase. For example, in 1967 the UK government devalued the pound from $2.80 to $2.40 – $1 bought 36 pence before the change and 42 afterwards (from 85 old pence to 100).

Governments could use exchange-rate devaluation to attempt to eliminate an unsustainable trade deficit. A devaluation would make imports more expensive in the national currency and exports cheaper in dollars, tending to reduce imports and increase exports. Jumping forward in time, we can note that when governments took their countries into the eurozone they lost this policy instrument.

For most advanced countries, manipulation of exchange rates for policy goals fell out of practice long before the advent of the eurozone. In 1971, with its gold reserves declining due to a falling trade balance and short-term financial outflow, the US government unilaterally ended the Bretton Woods System by terminating the link between the dollar and the price of gold. After considerable instability in exchange rates among countries, a new orthodoxy emerged. The new orthodoxy embraced the long-standing arguments of conservative ideologues that markets, not governments, should determine exchange rates.

The International Monetary Fund annually classifies country exchange rates. In 2018 it listed twenty-five governments as operating with "independently floating" exchange rates, which included almost every European and North American country, as well as Japan. A further fifty-one fell into the "managed floating with no predetermined path for the exchange rate" (IMF, *De facto Classification of Exchange Rate Regimes and Monetary Policy Framework*). In effect, the new orthodoxy decommissions the exchange rate as a policy instrument even for governments with national currencies.

In addition to removing from use an instrument for active economic management, leaving exchange-rate determination to capital markets facilitates financial speculation. The exchange rate is a price that has a major impact on a country's economy. The change from fixed to "floating" rates transfers control over that price from governments to the private sector.

Many, perhaps most, commentators, both expert and lay, argue that, once the US government ended the fixed gold price, fixed exchange rates became a prac-

tical impossibility. That argument has validity in that
a twenty-first-century global system of fixed exchange
rates would require agreement among the governments
of all major countries, what many call "a new Bretton
Woods." However, only ideology would prevent governments from managing exchange rates by the purchase
and sale of foreign exchange reserves. Since the Bretton
Woods System collapsed many governments have pur-
posefully managed their exchange rates.

But in practice the ideology of free markets has
removed exchange-rate intervention from the public
policy toolbox. When one suggests it, the reply comes
quickly: "That may once have been possible, but no
more." "There is no alternative" to leaving exchange
rates to global financial markets.

## Decommissioning Monetary Policy

One of the few progressive aspects of US economic
policy institutions is the legislatively mandated political oversight of the central bank, the Federal Reserve
System. Legislation requires the head of the Federal
Reserve to report regularly to Congress, which typically takes the form of testimony before a congressional
committee. In addition, the legislation creating the US
central bank states that the board of governors of the
Federal Reserve System has "fair representation of the
financial, agricultural, industrial, and commercial interests and geographical divisions of the country." More
important, the Federal Reserve System has a mandate
to consider employment as well as inflation: "to promote effectively the goals of maximum employment,

stable prices, and moderate long-term interest rates." In practice, the effectiveness of the political oversight has waxed and waned, depending on the chairman and the politics of the time.

Conventional wisdom holds that, in the final decades of the twentieth century, the power of central banks increased dramatically in almost all countries, including the United States. The truth is quite the opposite. The role of central banks in most countries, advanced and underdeveloped, narrowed substantially towards the end of the twentieth century. The vehicle for this narrowing was their so-called operational independence.

In the United Kingdom, Gordon Brown, Chancellor under the Labour government in 1997, ended the long-standing direct control of the Bank of England. This change in status included the creation of a "Monetary Policy Committee" (MPC), which, unlike in the United States, included putative experts and no members from business, trade unions or the public. In the European Union, the membership of the equivalent to the British MPC for the ECB comes from national central banks, with no participation by any representatives beyond financial bureaucracies.

This partial to complete insulation of central banks from democratic oversight draws justification from explicitly ideological arguments. Without independence, central bank decisions would fall prey to populist demands from government for reckless monetary expansion to fuel populist budget deficits. The doctrine of central bank independence is anti-democratic. The essence of the argument is that monetary policy is a technical matter and that any degree of democratic oversight results in reckless and irresponsible policies.

190

# Always an Alternative

Monetary decisions are not a matter for public involvement. They should be under the control of a technical or financial elite.

Allowing democracy to intrude on the decision making of central banks brings unsustainable inflation and the collapse of currencies. "There is no alternative" to leaving these decisions to the experts.

## Decommissioning Fiscal Policy

Fiscal policy was used by a few governments during the Great Depression of the 1930s, notably in the United States, in an ad hoc manner. The first clear legal commitment to an active fiscal policy was the US Full Employment Act of 1946, the preamble of which states:

> The [US] Congress hereby declares that it is the continuing policy and responsibility of the Federal Government to use all practicable means ... with the assistance and cooperation of industry, agriculture, labor, and State and local governments ... to promote maximum employment, production, and purchasing power.

In the early 1970s, conservatives in the economics profession initiated a critique of this legal commitment, developing an analytical decommissioning of fiscal policy. The basic argument to decommission fiscal policy was and is that it is unnecessary. It cannot contribute to employment, which would achieve its maximum possible value automatically through the adjustment of free markets. However, this is a rather weak argument against fiscal policy, if the economy is plagued by unemployment. The argument that an active fiscal policy is unnecessary

191

is reinforced by two mutually complementary arguments, that the unemployment one observes is almost entirely voluntary and that an active fiscal policy would make unemployment, voluntary or involuntary, worse.

Economists before the Great Depression of the 1930s argued that unemployment is the result of wages being too high. Just as a high price for apples leaves apples unsold, minimum wages and trade union pressure drive up wages and reduce the ability of business to employ people. This too is a weak argument in the twenty-first century, when the membership and economic strength of trade unions has declined in most advanced countries and problems of enforcement and erosion through inflation have undermined minimum wages.

Critics of fiscal policy find their next culprit for idle workers in unemployment compensation itself. Far from being a stabilizing program (see chapter 2), support for the unemployed reduces the incentive to seek work, an argument that would garner the Nobel Prize in Economics in 2010. The argument carries great political power, because it reinterprets involuntary loss of income as willing avoidance of work, which is made worse by well-meaning reforms.

Belief in free-market outcomes and benefit-induced unemployment combined to decommission fiscal policy. The argument goes that active fiscal measures, even if they were to reduce unemployment temporarily, are intrinsically undesirable. The argument against an active fiscal policy comes from three fallacies derived from the faith in free-market outcomes, all focusing on public-sector deficits: government spending reduces private expenditure, causes inflation and diminishes private-sector confidence.

192

Always an Alternative

The possibility that a fiscal expansion might directly reduce private expenditure, sometimes called "crowding out," allegedly results from a rise in interest rates. However, "crowding out" depends on how a fiscal expansion is financed and how businesses respond to interest rates. In a recession, idle capacity in the business sector makes the urge to invest quite low whatever the interest rate, which was obvious in all advanced economies after 2008. In any case, a government can completely avoid crowding out by financing expenditure with bond sales to the central bank.

We dealt with the "fiscal expansion causes inflation" argument in the previous chapter, which leaves the private-sector confidence argument, whose great strength lies in its vagueness, making it almost impossible to refute. In 2010 the Conservative British government presented this argument under the imaginatively oxymoronic title of an "expansionary fiscal contraction." The essence of this and similar arguments against fiscal policy is that a public-sector deficit and the debt it creates are themselves a direct cause of falls in private-sector "confidence," which undermines business investment. At the end of the 2000s and into the following decade, the marginally more plausible crowding-out argument could not be made because nominal interest rates were close to zero and could not fall further.

The more respectable version of this anti-deficit argument suggests that businesses and citizens consider that a fiscal deficit is equivalent to a future tax increase. To prepare for the tax increase they reduce their expenditures (called Ricardian equivalence by economists). Were this true, the increase in the individual tax burden would be very low, as well as discounted into the future.

193

All such arguments against public deficits and debt fail adequately to recognize that the public bonds held by the private sector are income-generating assets.

These ideological arguments against an active fiscal policy prompted political moves in the US Congress to restrict the federal government's flexibility to implement deficit finance, such as the Budget Enforcement Act of 1990. In the European Union we find far more draconian legal limitation on deficits, the "Excessive Deficit Procedure." This "procedure," which has treaty status, limits government budget deficits to below 3 percent of GDP and grants the European Commission powers to sanction governments that do not comply.

Legal restrictions on public-sector deficits, like central bank independence, remove fiscal policy from democratic decision making, however flawed that process may be. Its defenders present the decommissioning of fiscal policy as a technical measure, designed to prevent irresponsible politicians from embarking on "populist" vote-buying expenditure programs that undermine the general welfare. To prevent destabilizing decisions by governments, "there is no alternative" to limiting the democratic process. Reality is quite different, as the great crisis of 2008 showed. Private-sector behavior destabilizes economies and the public sector must intervene to restore order.

### There is an Alternative: Democracy

Through the dispelling of myths we have demonstrated that their power comes from repetition by politicians and the media, not from theoretical or empirical validity.

They are all based on ideology that calls into question the validity of public management of market economies. The fundamental issue in a democratic society is not whether inflation, deficits or unemployment are too high or too low. The fundamental issue is who decides? The general rule in democratic societies is that experts advise and democratically elected representatives decide. Collective decisions reached through a democratic process lay the basis for sound economic policies.

While democracy in many cases is associated with dysfunctional polices, the lack of democracy eliminates the citizen's power to alter policies. Whatever specific form democratic oversight might take, public knowledge of policy alternatives and how policies yield outcomes is essential. We can institutionalize public knowledge of economic policies by creating institutions to promote that knowledge.

A simple rule guides us to and through policy choices. In 1969 a Dutch economist, Jan Tinbergen, received the Nobel Prize in Economics. Of his many contributions to economic policy, the best remembered is the "Tinbergen Rule." The rule states that, to achieve all its goals, a government must have policy instruments equal to the number of those goals. For example, if our government seeks 1) full employment, 2) manageable inflation, 3) a sustainable balance on external transactions, and 4) lower inequality, it requires four different tools. These might be the fiscal balance to achieve the employment goal, monetary policy to manage inflation, exchange-rate invention for external balance, and progressive tax rates to reduce income disparities.

The TINA principle achieves plausibility by eliminating policy instruments. Restrict the deficit, insulate the central bank for democratic control, float the exchange rate, and replace direct taxes with indirect ones, and, surprise, there is no alternative to accepting what private markets dictate. But if we recommission those policy tools, there will always be, not one, but many alternatives for citizens to choose among. If we are denied access to the steering wheel, the brakes and the accelerator pedal, we have no alternative to accepting a private-sector chauffeur. We can change the rules and drive ourselves.

# Index

# Index

# Index

# Index

# Index

# Index

# Index

203

# Index

# Index

# Index

# Index

# Index

# Index